Still Small Voice

DAVID HILL

Names of both the innocent and guilty have been changed, omitted, or fictionalised. Descriptions of events have been adapted in part, for dramatic effect and may not have occurred exactly as described or in the exact sequences as described, or on the dates specified.

Copyright © 2021 David Hill

Published by StoryJug

All rights reserved.

ISBN: 979-8-7753-4287-6

This book is dedicated

to my wife, Lydia

CHAPTER 1

STILL SMALL VOICE

CHILDREN & YOUNG PERSONS ACT, 1969

NAME: David James Hill

NAME OF PARENT (in full): Mother – Rosalie Mary Hill

DATE OF BIRTH: 19.9.64   SEX: Male

ADDRESS: 91, Grassendale Avenue, North Prospect, Plymouth.

SCHOOL: Home Tutor

REPORTING OFFICER: P.C. 274 GILES
Date of offence: 21st July 1974

David Hill, with John NP, aged eight years, forcibly entered a store in Wolseley Road by smashing a window and inserting a hand through the hole to remove a bottle of lemonade.

Has not previously come to the notice of the police.

He is in fact under the age of criminal responsibility.

Submitted for information.

Burglary – one case.

Date of Offence: 21st July 1974

David Hill, with John NP, aged eight years, forcibly entered a store in Wolseley Road by smashing a window and inserting a hand through the hole to remove a bottle of lemonade.

Has not previously come to the notice of the police.

My five siblings all arrived before me. They are Christine, Stephen, Tony, Martin and Maureen. Growing up, I wasn't short of company, love or attention. By the time I was born, my brothers were already all wrong'uns. My dad, Les Hill, was not to blame. He was a grafter. But even with his love and protection, and his work ethic, his influence was no match for the excitements on offer in Harcliffe, the rough part of Bristol where we lived.

I hardly knew my dad. He was a road worker. His friends were all Irish navvies. When he took me to the pub with him, I'd sit on the floor and they'd all chuck coins at me. I remember him bringing a dog home once. That's a happy memory. I was about four then.

My mum and dad and both sets of grandparents came from Devon and Cornwall. Both grandfathers had spent their formative years serving king and country, dodging death in war zones. My mum was born in 1931. My dad was a little older. They were properly in love, and it gives me a warm glow to know that – that I come from love. My dad dodged death in the Second World War, getting shot in the leg and then summarily discharged. It's a wonder our family's here at all really, when you think of all the odds that were stacked against it.

I wished I'd known Dad for longer. I remember him as a strong, fit no-nonsense bloke, grounded in his own sense of justice. When one of our neighbours had a spat with our Stephen, my dad set to on him. "You touch my son and I'll blow your head off." He grabbed the man by his scruff and picked him up off the floor so his feet were dangling. My dad was protective but not violent, not usually, not as I remember him.

I think dads are very important, and now I am one, I've got a better feeling for what I missed out on, but back then? As the saying goes, you can't miss what you've never really had. I don't for an instant believe my dad could have prevented me or my brothers from getting into as much trouble as we did.

I remember Dad dying. I was five, nearly six years old. Thrombosis, they said. He was digging up a road. He stopped work and told his work pals he didn't feel too clever. They told him to go in the pub and grab a whisky. Dad dutifully went off to the pub but didn't get very far. He collapsed and never recovered consciousness again. An ambulance came and took him to hospital but he was dead by the time it got there. Some men came to the house to tell Mum what had happened.

Lots of people came to the house after that, to mourn with Mum. I remember asking where my dad had gone, because they were all talking about him. He's just gone, they said. I remember Mum crying – she wasn't one for crying. She usually just got on with things.

I was quite struck by it – having a dead father. I have a clear memory of when they all came back from the funeral (which I didn't attend); a throng of friends and neighbours all stood round the three-bar electric fire in our back room. I stood at a distance down the hallway and watched them. It seemed to me that the past was already spinning away from me before I'd even got a chance to look at it properly.

That was that then. Dad was gone and we were skint.

***

Next up the pecking order to me was our Maureen. She was seven going on eight when Dad died, our Tony *was* eight, Martin nine and Stephen eleven going on twelve. Christine was ten years older than Stephen and not my father's child, not that this made much difference to us, or Dad even. After he died she emigrated to South Africa. She'd been planning the move for some time. Alone with four boys and a young daughter to look after, Mum could have done with all the help she could get, but she wouldn't and didn't ask any of us to share her burden, and she wouldn't have prevented her eldest child from embarking on the adventure of a lifetime. After Christine left for South Africa, we became estranged from her but not disconnected. She is and always will be one of us.

Having to raise five children without help or money pushed Mum over the edge a few times. She had breakdowns. She collapsed on the stairs once. They carted her off to hospital but brought her home again the same day. Mum wouldn't leave us on our own. And she couldn't have seen any one of us go into care.

None of us were very helpful. In fact, we made things worse, much worse. We brought the police to the house frequently. Her life was a constant round of cooking, washing, working and worry, with sleep coming in a poor fifth. Her life was us. She never stopped caring for us. If she had dark days... no, I can't say "if" – *when* she had dark days, she didn't trouble us with them. Truth is, we never bothered to find out how well she was coping. We just took it for granted she would.

***

With Harcliffe being so rough, we boys had to learn to defend ourselves from early on. Mum had neither the time nor the wherewithal to fight our battles or prevent us from starting any. Whilst I was often stuck at home, and still very young, my brothers went off on their adventures without me. I waited patiently to get up to speed and go with them. Once we were out the house, we pretty much did as we pleased. My brothers were all expert shoplifters. I carried out my first job at four years old, sliding a haul of Mars Bars into my little red wellies. It was easy. And it would be just as easy to blame our wickedness on the grief we all felt after losing Dad so suddenly. Truth is, Dad was still with us when, even me at four years old, we were all out there, bang at it.

***

With Christine gone, Maureen was the only sibling who didn't turn to crime for excitement and entertainment and who consequently didn't bring any trouble home. A couple of years older than me, Maureen has never committed any crime nor shown any desire to. She has spent her life caring for people.

From an early age then, I had a lot on and a lot to learn. To keep up with my brothers, I had to be fast and agile. Physically, I was a slight lad with a Donny Osmond baby face and long curly hair. Throughout my childhood I was often mistaken for a girl. All I wanted was to be a man, to grow up fast, to be strong.

***

A couple of years after Dad died, Mum finally conceded that the scale of the task confronting her was too great for one woman to cope with. She needed help. She had a sister who lived in Devon who offered, but only if Mum would up sticks and move. Aunty Jean had no wish to live in Harcliffe. I doubt anyone ever has. So we left Bristol to live by the sea in Plymouth.

***

We moved, Dad-less, into a lovely house in a district of Plymouth called Pennycross. If there was a wrench, I didn't feel it. But Mum must have. And my brothers.

Flung so far from the little house we'd called home, we bonded as one unit. Mum may have had too many troubles to count, but she had no reason to worry about our love for each other as a family. We were all silent about our sadness, but we were solid. Close.

Our new house had four bedrooms and grass and a shed. That's how I remember it. I'd just turned seven years old when we got there. My school was just round the corner, Pennycross Primary. It was bright and airy, and though the sea wasn't too far away, we spent much of our time in school drawing it and talking about it: Drake and the Armada, fishing boats, the great Gog and Magog. We never got to clap eyes on it. Some days you could even smell it.

That said, Pennycross Primary was far and away a better place to be than the school I'd left behind in Harcliffe. There was no need to be vigilant here, to be in a state of constant defence. One of my best (and only) memories of this school was playing a donkey in the Nativity play. I removed my donkey's head at the end of the performance and felt a warm glow spread across my face when I saw my mother, sitting alone on the front row, looking up at me and clapping.

Every day I walked to school with a boy called Steven who lived around the corner from me. It was the first real friendship I cultivated on my own terms and the only one that could be described as innocent and ordinary. We sat in class together. We climbed trees, shared sweets, built dens, all proper kid's stuff. I climbed trees right to the top, always. Steve would stand underneath sucking his thumb, looking up at me. That's how I remember him, looking up to me.

At home, we were swimming in space and spoilt for bedrooms. I shared a bedroom with my brother Tony. He, like my other brothers Martin and Stephen, went out on the rob frequently – and mitched school even more frequently. I was privy to their secret stashes and hordes of loot. I heard them tell stories and make plans. I ached to go with them on a shout so I could share in this excitement.

"You're too young," they kept saying.

***

Though we were now living in the same town as Aunty Jean, it didn't feel like we were any closer to her. Without transport, it was a day's work to go and see her. So Mum put in for another council house transfer. Before the stamp was dry on the envelope, we were given a three-bedroom house in a place called Swilly, and the name of the place should tell you why our request for an exchange was granted so rapidly. They tried to re-brand Swilly as North Prospect just after we got there, but even today people still refer to the lowlifes who live there as "them from Swilly". I still live there.

If you live in Swilly and you hear that someone in Pennycross wants to swap with you, you call the removal van the same day and park outside their house before they get a chance to change their minds, which is exactly what happened.

After enjoying the ecstasy and freedom of a clean spacious house in a safe and sunny setting, amongst friends who just wanted to have fun, we arrived in Swilly with the kind of thump you get when the bottom falls out of your rust-bucket motor car. Didn't matter though. Mum was happy. She could walk to Aunty Jean's and have a cup of tea with her every day of the week if she wanted to.

***

Coming from Harcliffe, my brothers and I knew how to defend ourselves and our territory, so we slotted into Swilly just fine, with minimal disruption or dissension from the hard-core criminals growing up there.

I shared a bedroom with different brothers at different times – depending on who was in borstal and who'd been let out. As a result, I got to learn a lot more about thieving than your average seven-year-old and, importantly, the kinds of strategies to use to prevent getting caught.

[*A note on names*: as in Pennycross, my first friend in Swilly was also called Steve, and in this book, he shall hereafter be known as "Bad" Steve. He was a lot more fun than Good Steve. He didn't want to ride bikes and climb trees. My brother Stephen was even worse than Bad Steve and could easily pass for Mad Steve, but he wouldn't like to be called that. To help you understand who's who, we'll call my brother Stephen from now on.]

STILL SMALL VOICE

One day, I found my old friend Good Steve from Pennycross on the doorstep.

"What do *you* want?" I wasn't pleased to see him. I don't know why, but him standing there – on my doorstep, goody two shoes – well it just wound me up.

I'd not long ago finished a set of bow and arrows I'd made out of fishing twine and branches of oak we'd collected from the woods nearby. The twine was orange, bendy and strong, and perfect for shooting with. I'd whittled the branches into sticks for arrows and then attached two-inch nails to the end of them, sharpened to deliver maximum impact. My arrows were heavy enough to gain speed on propulsion but not so heavy as to render the bow itself useless. They delivered perfect flight for my needs. I'd been working on them all week and had finished more than a dozen.

He was rocking back and forth on the doorstep, like he wanted to come in.

"'Ang on there a minute," I told him. I went and got my bow and filled my arrow holder – an empty cut-down *Fairy Liquid* bottle pierced with holes for the string to go through – full of arrows. I slipped this over my shoulder and set off.

"Come on," I said to him. I shut the front door behind us. "Let's go play cowboys and injuns."

As soon as we were out on the street, I told him to get off home.

"Eh?"

"Go on," I said. "Get off back to Pennycross. We don't want you round 'ere."

"But I thought I was your friend?" he said.

"I've already got a friend called Steve," I told him. "I don't need two, so fuck off back to where you came from. Go on."

As he walked away from me, down the street, I took an arrow from my pot, aimed and shot. It hit him in the leg and stuck there. Blood poured. He looked terrified, which only encouraged me. He ran, and so I ran after him. I could see the arrow wiggling about in his flesh as he ran. He was hobbling now, trying to hold onto the arrow in his leg, not sure whether to pull it out. I shot another two arrows, aiming for his back. Both arrows struck him. They were stuck into his back, one each side, landing as I'd dreamt they would. Blood leaked from the wounds, generously. I was really impressed by the effect, the impact, the result. It felt good. The last memory I have of my good friend Steve is a picture of him running away from me, looking back with the face of a man condemned.

I didn't stop at bow and arrows. I made boomerangs with blades at the end, so sharp, if you weren't careful they'd have your fingers off. I knocked out the front three teeth of a boy called Kevin whose mother was so stunned by my wanton cruelty she made it her mission to ensure her son would never cross my path again. Probably wisely. Most of the boys in my neighbourhood were a bit slow to catch on to the fact they would be in peril if they crossed me.

Much of the city of Plymouth had been bombed during the war, and so, like kids all over England, we played on the bleak grey fields and wasteland set aside for new builds. Our dens were underground, and mine had little steps leading down into it. To hide it, at the end of a day, we filled in the opening so no one could find it and take it over. Me and this boy Bradley were going at it with shovels, creating cover, until we got to a point where I figured it'd be safe enough.

"Stop it now, Bradley. We're there." I stood on my shovel as I'd seen my dad stand on his. I knew this game. I knew this game more than Bradley would ever know it.

"No, there's loads to do yet," he said.

Something must have snapped inside me.

"Stop it, Bradley, or I'll hit you with this shovel."

He carried on.

"One more time and that's it."

You see, I think a sensible kid would just do as they're told. But no. Bradley wanted to test my nerve. I hit him over the head with the shovel. *Boing*. I can still hear it now.

He fell face down on top of the den. I pulled him off but he didn't move. I waited a couple of minutes, but nothing. No movement. I looked around. No one. I was going to just leave him there but decided instead to tell Mum. She came out to see him, my brothers in tow. Fifteen minutes passed and he was still lying there. Just as I began to panic, he came round. He stood up and started running round in circles, shouting, "I'll get you, I'll get you." And then he ran off down the road.

He turned out to be the only child in his family who didn't turn into a heroin addict. I used to wonder about that – just a co-incidence I'm sure.

***

Plymouth had a zoo back in the early seventies. A proper zoo with lions and elephants, bears and monkeys, giraffes, zebras and cheetahs. The works. It was sited on Central Park, next to Plymouth Argyle's football ground. It took up what is now a huge swathe of green surrounded by housing estates. Bowing to pressure, Mum took us there one Saturday, and whilst there she bought us sweets and drinks from a hut in the middle of the main walking area. It was a rickety old thing and so dead easy to break into. The same night, after we'd gone to bed, Tony and Martin decided they'd go and rob it.

"If you don't take me, I'll tell," I said. "And I mean it."

The zoo was quite high up Central Park, and you could see Plymouth Hoe from it. I saw a big moon looming over the ocean. The sea looked like cling film, creased. The silence of the night was in constant flux, being interrupted with grunts and birdsong, monkey screams and digging noises.

We filled our pockets with Toffee Crisps and Crunchies, Sherbet Fountains and Mars Bars. Tony ransacked the place for the petty cash box, a red metal box with the key still in it and full of coppers.

We left the hut and stood in front of it, chomping on chocolate.

The zoo in the moonlight was a devilish place to be. The lion was behind a double enclosure, but they're big when you're only seven and there are no grown-ups around. He just opened one eye at us. The bears were still pacing as I'd seen them that very morning. The polar bears were gleaming in the moonlight. We woke the black bears – I know they were black bears because that morning I'd counted them. There were eight. They stood up and lined their cage, looking out at us. Their eyes were full of sadness. Glistening. I didn't like them.

We wandered home, chatting quietly to one another, chomping on what sweets we had left. It was my first successful robbery.

***

We had fourteen steps on the stairs in our house. To get down them, I'd launch myself off the landing and fly, trying to clear as many steps as I could before grabbing the handrail. By the time I was eight years old, I was clearing ten. The day after the night at the zoo, I tried for eleven but landed very badly. The pain was excruciating. I said nothing to no one. I'd been suffering with pain in my leg for a while – a deep and sickening pain that ran all the way down my leg, emanating from my hip. It had been going on for weeks and I'd been ignoring it. After failing to clear the eleventh stair, this pain got worse, much worse. I did now think that perhaps it was a sign that something more serious was going on.

One day, when I was on my way up to St Budeaux to see a friend, the pain was so overwhelming it took me down. I collapsed in the middle of a main road, unconscious to the danger I was in. Luckily the traffic stopped, an ambulance was called and I awoke to find myself in hospital with my mum, staring at a wall full of X-rays.

The X-rays revealed the extent of the damage, which hadn't been caused by stair jumping, as I'd imagined, but by sheer bad luck. I was suffering from a condition called Perthes' disease, named for the man who discovered it. Where the head of the thigh bone should be rounded to fit snugly into the socket of the hip bone, so creating a moving joint allowing a fluid walking movement, the end of my leg bone had softened and crumbled, and so it didn't fit any more. My bone was so badly damaged they wouldn't let me go home. They wheeled me around the hospital, here, there and everywhere. I felt like I'd been captured – tricked into jail. Knowing they were doing their best for her son, my mother didn't put up much of a fight for me. She didn't argue with them. On the contrary, I think she was pleased to get me out of her hair for a few days. But it wasn't going to be a few days. They – the hospital screws as I saw them – were planning on keeping me bedbound, weighed down, literally, by a pulley of metal blocks so I was stuck fast to my bed and completely immobile, for eleven long weeks. And as if that wasn't enough, they sealed my fate and closed off any chance of my escape by putting a wooden bar across my legs and then containing me in a box made from plaster of Paris, with only my head and feet showing from each end of it. Not even at that age could I have risked being seen out and about on the streets of Swilly wearing such a thing. I was stuck to my bed, trapped, not happy. Getting bathed, going to the loo... it was a living hell. Over the next eleven weeks they practised all kinds of torture on me.

Only gradually did they reduce the size and complexity of the many and various torture devices they tried out on me. They swapped the plaster of Paris suit of armour for a more permanent girdle, a rigid and robust plastic straitjacket that could incorporate my whole torso and hips. This new apparatus also ensured that any agile or spontaneous frolics or excitements that would quite naturally spring forth from the soul of a child as spirited as I was, didn't. So even though I was allowed to stand up, they caged me.

On the day I left the hospital, they decided to heap yet more humiliation upon me by giving me yet one more Houdini-style challenge to contend with. They asked me to stand on my good leg and to bend my bad leg up, as if ready to give someone a good kicking. They then attached a dog collar and leather rope round the ankle of my bent bad leg and connected this to the girdle I was wearing round my body. Trussed up, so to speak. I felt like a bird being prepared for the oven. They did all this to make me look like an idiot, to discourage me from playing out with my mates. They claimed their aim was to position my thigh so that that ball and socket of my hip bone grew into one other at the right angle. And to stop me falling over they gave me a pair of crutches. Bye, David. See ya!

I couldn't go to school and had no wish to. They sent someone round to teach me at home. They came for a few hours every week for two years. I wasn't interested. They had me back and forth to the hospital every other day having X-ray after X-ray, injections, operations, medication, physio and full-on big arguments with doctors. I was frustrated and aggrieved but more pained by the loss of my freedom than the actual physical affliction.

Only by keeping my leg hitched up to the girdle could I keep the ball of my thigh inside the socket of my hip bone. The doctors described this as "our" challenge for the next few years. But it wasn't "our" challenge, it was "mine". I had to walk around with my leg hitched up to this girdle until I was fourteen years old.

I was nearly ten years old and still on crutches when I was captured by the police for the very first time. For stealing a bottle of lemonade.

CHAPTER 2

DEVON AND CORNWALL CONSTABULARY   Form 121a

CHILDREN & YOUNG PERSONS' ACT, 1969

: David James Hill

NAME OF PARENT (in full): Mother – Rosalie Mary Hill

DATE OF BIRTH: 19.9.64   SEX: Male

ADDRESS: 91, Grassendale Avenue, North Prospect, Plymouth.

FAMILY: Father dead, lives with mother

SCHOOL: Camel's Head Secondary Modern

EMPLOYMENT:

REPORTING OFFICER: PC 1060 CLEMENS

Date of offence: 27.10.76

Circumstances: Deliberate damage to children's swings in Cookworthy Road, North Prospect by setting fire to the plastic seats, thereby causing damage to the value of £20. He has, in fact, denied this offence despite some evidence to the contrary.

Home conditions do not appear to be very satisfactory, and I am aware that this family is well known to your department.

Has come to the notice of police on one previous occasion, i.e. 21.7.74 – burglary – but police took no further action in view of the fact he was underage.

Process being considered. Criminal damage one case.

My trouble-making brothers are writ large throughout my childhood memories. Our Stephen, nearly six years older than me, couldn't walk down the street without threatening someone. He was no good at eye contact. Out of all of my brothers, he disturbed me the most in that he lacked the candour and control of serious criminals who know when and whether a fight's worth having. Nevertheless, I idolised him. Dark, with big brown eyes, he always wore a feather cut hairstyle and flared trousers. He had a nervous grin that used up every muscle in his face but didn't express any sense of joy or happiness. Like an elastic band stretched to its full capacity, an offhand comment or a sideways glance from someone was incentive enough for him to snap. "Volatile" was how the police described him. Everyone else just knew to steer clear of him.

My mother had her work cut out. She was driven to meet our every need, cooking and cleaning, from daybreak to bedtime. She had no time for herself, and no inclination to upset us with a firm hand and threats of violence. With no man about the house, the vacancy was filled by our Stephen, who at thirteen years old was in no rush to learn a range of parenting skills, preferring instead to concentrate his efforts on the use of fear and physical punishment. Our Martin and Tony took the brunt of his discipline regime because I was still just a kid. When he wasn't home, which thankfully was more the norm, then our Stephen was a fully employed and highly successful jewel thief. He robbed in broad daylight. He took jewels by sleight of hand. He posed as a buyer. Yes. At thirteen years old. *"Could I just have a look at that gold chain please? Oh, and that one there behind you."* He hid his hauls, or "parcels" as we called them, all over the house, in the loft, behind the washing machine, even inside my girdle, when he knew the police were due round.

Tony was the brother closest to me in age, by three years or so. In another life he might have been a teacher. He taught me hallmarks and carats and how to spot a decent carriage clock. Being pinned to a sofa for a very long time, I had a lot of time to digest all this information.

Martin was very straightforward, but like Tony, he lacked the ambition and spirit of a real villain, a trait neither Stephen nor I were short of. Martin did as he was told and performed well. Good at logistics, he was punctual, organised and cool. But not much of a dreamer. With Stephen in charge, my three brothers worked well together. There were never any fights about the work. We were a close family, and we accepted each other's talents and flaws as given. If and when we did fight, it was usually about jackets and shirts and how much meat we had on our plate. We've always been strong on loyalty but not so keen to show any kind of physical affection towards each other.

***

EXTRACT FROM REPORT TO

PLYMOUTH JUVENILE COURT

20th April 1977

CONCERNING: David James Hill

D.O.B: 19.9.64

OFFENCES: Theft and criminal damage.

PREVIOUS: Burglary – no further action taken because of age.

Family:
Father   Deceased
Mother   Rosalie Mary Hill – housewife
Siblings: Stephen Hill
                          Martin Hill
                          Anthony Hill
                          Maureen Hill
                          David James Hill

Home:

This family took up residence at their present home in December 1972. The Hills moved to Plymouth from Bristol in April 1972 and lived in a four-bedroomed house in Fountains Crescent. The present home is a three-bedroomed semi-detached house which was redecorated and refurbished three years ago by the housing department. It is fairly clean and tidy and the rent is £1.34 per week with rebates.

Concerned:

David is the youngest in the family. The family have had their troubles in the past. David attended Pennycross Primary School until he was eight years old. When David was seven years old, his hip was damaged, and at the age of eight years he was withdrawn from school and remained at home receiving home tuition for two years. He made some educational progress but his home tutor commented that David would have to return to a normal school setting to receive an all-round education. David eventually returned to school last year and commenced at Camel's Head. His attendance record is good and he seems to like the school. David attends no youth club, preferring to use his spare time fishing or riding his bicycle. He receives fifty pence pocket money per week.

Offences:

This is not the first time David has come to the notice of the police. On 21st July 1974 David was involved in a burglary but no further action was taken because of his age. Today he is being charged with theft of a cigarette lighter and damage to children's swings. David admits to stealing the lighter, which was later recovered. He states that he had nothing to do and therefore he stole the lighter. However, he is denying the second charge of setting fire to the children's swings. He states that two other boys did the damage and he was merely an onlooker.

General observation:

Mrs Hill seems to be a fairly hard-working mother but her control over her sons and daughter is definitely slackening. She does not understand why David has become involved in crime and tells me that he is usually very well behaved and helpful around the house. Mrs Hill has a boyfriend who seems to be very involved with her but seems to have little influence over the children's discipline. Nevertheless, there is good family time between the members of the household.

Conclusion:

It would appear that, following the example of his older brothers, David is now experimenting with crime. David does know the difference between right and wrong and seems to be, like a lot of children within his environment, unable to give a real reason for committing crime. I would therefore recommend that Your Worships consider that the best way of dealing with this young man would be to give him a monetary penalty and an attendance centre order.

Signed: Peter Gilbert, Social Worker

Devon County Council

Social Services Department

I was given a supervision order, which meant having social workers "popping round" to keep an eye on me. The following is just a selection of some of the reports that were made as a result of the supervision order.

DEVON COUNTY COUNCIL SOCIAL SERVICES DEPARTMENT

Where seen, general appearance	Plymouth Juvenile Court
Were child and foster parent/caring person seen alone?	No
Condition of clothing	Very good
Condition of home (including bedroom and sleeping arrangements):	Very clean, tidy and well furnished
Health: Doctor:	Seemingly good
School or employment:	Camel's Head Sec. Modern
Contact with relatives, parents and foster parents'/caring persons' attitude to relatives:	Lives with mother, sister and brother

Friends, hobbies, activities	Normal play
Religious training	C of E

PLYMOUTH NORTH DIVISION: STATUTORY VISIT REPORT

NAME OF CHILD: David James Hill
Address: 91, Grassendale Avenue, Plymouth

NAME OF PARENT: Mrs Hill

DATE OF VISIT: **20.4.77 11 am**

TYPE OF CASE: **SUPERVISION ORDER**

Excerpts from a selection of reports from subsequent visits, in accordance with the supervision order.

General Report 20.4.77 – 11 am

David appeared before the Plymouth Juvenile Court today (20.4.77) on a charge of theft and criminal damage. (Report by Mr P. Gilbert S/W). He was made the subject of a supervision order for two years. I explained to the lad in the presence of his mother the nature and purpose of the order, and advised him of the likely consequences of any further breaches of the law, etc. Unfortunately, he has seen his brothers

Stephen and Martin committed to borstal training in the past.

Mrs Hill is a very pleasant woman and tries very hard to keep a good home.

General Report 27.5.77 – 8.15 am

On arrival I found David having breakfast together with Anthony, who has now left school. Mrs Hill was busily "hoovering" through the house. The lad was well clothed, clean and tidy. He stated that he was quite well, keeping out of trouble. Mrs Hill added that she was trying hard to keep him away from "bad company". David spoke of school with some enthusiasm, and I again reminded him of the real need for him to keep out of trouble.

General Report 15.9.77 – 5.30 pm

David was at home with a friend and his brother, the latter being home (so he said) for a day or so. Mrs Hill was out so I saw David in the kitchen on his own. The lad stated that he was quite happy and was trying to keep out of trouble. Unfortunately, both brothers have been to borstal, and whilst his mother always seems to cooperate, it may well be that she will find it difficult to offset the influence of David's brothers. I *advised the lad to ensure that he kept out of trouble and the likely consequences if he didn't.*

General Report 19.10.77 5 pm

Mrs Hill was out when I called, but on my second visit at 5 pm, David answered the door. As his mother was out, I spoke to him on the front doorstep. He stated he was quite happy and was keeping out of bother. It appears that he rarely goes out. On the school front, he has started to take an interest in rugby, although it is not played on a regular basis. David is also keen on football. I again advised him of the real need to keep out of trouble, which the lad may find difficult as both his elder brothers have already spent a period at borstal.

***

The excitement of going to big school wore off quickly. Even though I was on crutches (they called me *Crutches*), I didn't fear the bullies when I did bother to go. I was a protected species. My brother Stephen was known and feared by all at Camel's Head Sec, or the Collij of Nollij as we called it. I never had to fight my corner, and by extension, neither did Bad Steve (Stephen T). As for learning, they couldn't have made the lessons any more boring if they'd sat down and tried their best to work out how to do just that.

Mum had quite a few jobs over the years. She worked as a waitress in a cafe in town during the day and down at the laundry early evening. There was always food in the house and clean clothes, ironed, folded and put away in our drawers. Our Stephen also went to work every day. He'd begun to investigate the jewellery shops further afield, over in Torquay. He'd let me get my glass magnifier on the gold he brought home so I could learn the hallmarks. He sold his gold to men in town who sold it on to men in Bristol and London. It could never be traced back.

***

DEVON AND CORNWALL CONSTABULARY

CHILDREN & YOUNG PERSONS' ACT, 1969

DATE: 3rd March, 1978

NAME: HILL David James

NAME OF PARENT/GUARDIAN (in full)): Mother - Rose Mary Hill

DATE OF BIRTH: 19.9.64   SEX: Male

ADDRESS: 91, Grassendale Avenue, North Prospect, Plymouth.

FAMILY: Natural parents

SCHOOL: Camel's Head Secondary Modern

EMPLOYMENT:

REPORTING OFFICER: P.C 2395 KOPINSKI

Date of offence: 26 and 30th of January 1978

Location of the offence: Bridewell Lane North, Western Mill, Plymouth,

With others: Stephen T

This boy stands reported for two joint offences of theft as follows:

1. On 26th of January, 1978 with S.T, he stole a quantity of ice cream and chocolate flakes the property of Williams Pure Ices Ltd.to the value of £34.
2. On 30 January, 1978 with S.T.he stole a quantity of sweets, chocolates and soft drinks the property of William's pure ices Ltd, to the value of £25.48 p.
All recovered.

He has one previous finding of guilt.

20.4.77 Plymouth Juvenile Court - Theft - 2 year supervision order.

Process recommended.

We quite frequently went over to Western Mill to burgle the ice cream factory. This place was an oasis amidst a landscape of crowded houses and a sprawling mass of gunmetal grey – the dockyard. It was the ambition of any lad who could hold a ruler straight to get a job in the dockyard, and once in there, put his feet up till pension time. At thirteen years old, the very prospect seemed too bleak to me, as bleak as the lake of industry and construction I looked down upon from the high spots of St Budeaux. Once we'd got in the factory and out again, we'd take our plunder and lie out on the grasslands at the side of the road, eating until we were sick. The spread of the dockyard was especially bleak on a sunny afternoon with a five-litre box of raspberry ripple to get through. We'd just eat and eat, hypnotised by the zum, zum, zum of the dockyard traffic that passed before us, the workers clutching their steering wheels, themselves hypnotised by traffic lights dictating their stop go, stop go, stop go.

CHAPTER 3

STILL SMALL VOICE

As a kid, most of my evenings were spent roaming the streets of Swilly. Being on crutches didn't limit my sense of adventure any. Nosy neighbours tend to look for trouble through their front windows, so when I first started robbing houses, I carved out recce routes, surveying potential quarry from the back. We'd wait until dark and go on the rampage, house to house. We flew over fences, up and down entries, in and out of sheds, from one backyard to the next. We were fast but vigilant, checking for lights, people, signs of wealth, easy access.

One night, we nearly got caught by a man who emerged out of his shed, so we legged it over his fence and the fences of the next two houses along. Johnny T. was ahead of me. I could hear him shouting for me from the next garden. I found him standing up against the window of a bungalow.

"We've got one 'ere. No one in," he whispered. "Come on."

The windows were wood and easy to prise open with a screwdriver. We got in through the back kitchen but went straight into the front room to close all the curtains. Wall-to-wall Christmas decorations and a tree. We put the tree lights on and settled down on the floor to open all the presents. There wasn't one gift worth stealing. All of it was rubbish.

Socks. A tie. Rubbish jumper. Sewing set. Clothes brush set. Not one thing. No jewellery.

Aside from the Christmas presents and the furniture, the smell told you straight away that this was an old person's place. In the main bedroom, on the dressing table, we found an Albert chain in the jewellery box but not much else. Just before we left, we tried the kitchen cupboards. Top shelf. Biscuit tin. Bingo. £49.00. We jumped for joy then, literally, grinning and gasping at the fortune we'd made. We'd never had so much money. This would be the first of many successful house jobs, hundreds.

***

After getting a taste of the rewards on offer in exchange for so little effort, the idea of getting a job as a paper boy didn't hold much merit for me. Working out how to get my hands on easy money seemed to be a better and more profitable way to use my imagination. My adventures were limited only by the constraints forced on me by my height (I was too small to drive cars) and my disability (I couldn't get far or go fast on crutches).

I learned my trade through hard work and a conscientious and consistent approach to the fundamental rules of crime. I was always alert for opportunity. I paid close attention to *unusual* police activity. I learned who to trust and how far. Sometimes I worked alone, other times I took help, but I was always in charge.

After my £49 biscuit tin success, instead of going to school every day, I'd wake up and make my way to the nearest empty house I knew was likely to yield a good result. I worked with lots of different people over the years, but more often than not, my partner in crime was Bad Steve, who didn't even like burgling that much. He just hated being at school without me even more.

Every day was work. Get up. Find a house. Burgle it. Sell the stuff on. Go to bed. Get up. Burgle. Sell. Bed. Get up. Burgle. Bed. Burgle. Burgle. Burgle. Shop for clothes and sweets and/or maybe go to a restaurant. The waiters in *Lanterns* got used to us in the end, but the first time we went in there, the manager came over to ask us if we had the money after we ordered steak Diane at £8 a hit and two beers. I took £700 in cash from my pocket and slammed it on the table. He walked away. That we were small children drinking lager had gone right over his head. We had cash – and could be easily relieved of it.

I approached each burglary with discipline, sticking to basic rules to give myself an optimum chance of success. Loosely, my MO went as follows:

(1) Assess if the house is worth robbing...

Every day, I was out on patrol. I made detailed observations and accrued a wealth of information to help manage risk and make decisions that would be profitable. I looked through windows, lots of them, and usually of houses without net curtains. At night, I made a mental note of which houses weren't lit up. If the house was dark and empty, I'd look in to see how they lived, how they fixed their furniture. What did they put on their mantelpiece? What did they leave out on the coffee table? What clocks did they have? Was the garden done nicely or was it a bit slapdash? What kind of gates did they use? How did they cut their bushes? There were many ways to tell if a house was worth robbing. A burglar alarm in a built-up area was sufficient to deter me, but in a well-to-do neighbourhood where the houses were far apart it wouldn't make much difference. I was usually on the lookout for clues that were more banal, like a tarted-up front door on a house in a poor neighbourhood. I made the not unreasonable assumption that such a person would probably have a couple of pieces of jewellery they were proud of too – well worth a visit. I looked at the *way* people painted their windows and how their curtains were presented. Some people are exuberant in the way they display their wealth – rose gold chains left on a table or a windowsill, a Hunter watch on the sideboard, a grandfather clock – a carriage clock on the mantelpiece was always a good sign. I'd built up a fair amount of expertise on the character and worth of different types of carriage clocks and so had a decent eye for them. Brass casing, a must. Pre-1900s French were my favourites, with the double button on top, a repeater for chimes and a wind-up. No quartz, no batteries, eight-day wind-ups and repeaters, they were the minimum. It's a very personal thing really, how to tell if a house is worth it – you just get a feeling. After looking at what's on offer, I would then turn my mind to security.

(2) Make sure there's no one in before going for it...

Some owners were especially cautious and used audio tapes of dogs barking to deter people like me. This strategy worked, but not because I was taken in. I just figured such types to be a bit too unpredictable and so not worth messing with. Leaving a light on in a room no one sits in is a dead giveaway – whenever I saw a landing light left on for two nights on the trot, that was like an open invitation to rob the place. Likewise a blinking telly that never gets turned off. All these tricks were well known and useful in aiding my decision to go for it. As a rule, I robbed any house that showed promise and then I worried about security after I was in there. Sometimes I made mistakes. I've burgled jewels from a bedside table while the owners were in bed, snoring, oblivious. I enjoyed that – the way time stood still in that very moment. The hand reaching over. The snore. The sleeping eyelids like tiny moons, quivering, as fragile as the silence I worked in. I enjoyed the rush of blood, the trick, the cheek of it. I enjoyed it a lot.

(3) Get myself inside without being watched, caught... or worse, attacked...

I was usually in and out within minutes, which is why a belled-up house in a remote location didn't pose any problems for me. I'd be long gone before the police arrived on the scene. More often than not I'd be watching them blue lighting their way to the "incident" as I made my way from it on the other side of the road.

To get into a house, I'd first of all leave my shoes under a hedge in the garden and swap them for black Chinese slippers, which you could buy for next to nothing off the market back then. I always had a pair rolled up in my pocket. Not only did they give me good "creepability", but afterwards I could sling them in a bin without attracting attention. I always made sure there was never any forensic evidence left on my feet. I also bought myself supple and tight-fitting Corgi leather gloves. I'd lose them frequently, one here, one there, and have to go back and buy more. I always bought them off the same girl in House of Fraser. I wonder if *she* ever wondered what I was doing with them all?

After donning slippers and gloves, I was ready to burgle. I carried a selection of break-in tools to help me lift window latches or prise open doors. I never carried too many tools, to avoid being classed as "going equipped" if caught. I took the bare essentials for making a clean entry and exit, and with the emphasis on "clean". With the aid of an automatic centre punch, you could lift a latch easy enough after making a hole in the window. A clothes peg was just as useful though – you could use the wire from a peg to turn a key in a Chubb lock in seconds with a bit of practice. When I found a door not bolted all the way down, I'd push my foot against it, grab the sides and exert pressure till it popped open. Lots of old doors could be opened like that. And windows.

(4)   Find an escape route out again…

The cardinal rule for me was to break in and double lock the front door straight away. If and when I took someone along with me, I'd use them as a lookout. As soon as I broke in, I'd go upstairs and check the back windows for drainpipe access, my escape route out of there. The job didn't end there of course. If there was a getaway car, I'd want to know exactly where it was parked so I could run straight to it, jump in and go. *Without* all these plans in place, I considered myself at serious risk of capture.

I often got disturbed by the owners midway through a burglary – that was unpleasant. One time, I was rifling through the drawers of someone's bedroom when I heard them coming up the stairs. This shouldn't happen. If the front door is double locked and the owners do come back, you get good notice of their arrival because they can't get their key in – you can hear them at the door, struggling and complaining. But some doors don't allow for this, and on this particular job, such was the case.

There were two of them, a man and a woman. They were so quiet, so very quiet. They'd got in through the front door and were on the stairs before I'd even sussed they were in the house! They were creeping up, towards me, stair by stair. They *knew* I was in there. I heard the rustle of their coats against the wall as they climbed, the creak of the wood, their breathing. I was stuck, frozen, listening to them. I could hear their fear even though my heart was thumping. I couldn't think straight. I soon came to my senses though and jumped out of the window just before they got inside the room. I clung onto a drainpipe and was down it and on the ground in seconds. I looked up and saw the man put his head through the window as I hopped my way out of his garden and back to Martin's car.

Close calls. There were so many. Once I was walking round houses searching for a target when I heard someone following me. I hid behind a wall wielding a golf club. That could have turned out nasty, but didn't. And that *was* unusual. I had no interest in using violence on a job. The pickings were never so rich to warrant the risk of a seven-year stretch getting them.

Not much put me off or scared me back then, but dogs did. I wouldn't rob a house with big dogs prowling round it. After one job, I nearly got caught. The alarms had gone off and the police arrived quickly, sirens blaring, a pack of dogs on hand to chase after me. I didn't like that. To change my appearance, I buried my coat – a good coat that I wanted to hang onto – and then ran off into the nearest street where I could blend in easily with the general public. Next day, I went back to retrieve the jacket and it had gone. They'd dug it up and taken it. That hurt. The chase, the lost coat... it all coalesced into a trauma of sorts, a kind of bruising. I became so freaked out about dogs I decided to take a Rambo knife out on jobs with me after that. A few weeks later, the jitters subsided and I came to my senses. I continued on with my career but I left the knife at home.

(5) *Do the burglary – find cash and valuables and leave again very quickly, carrying away as many valuables as possible.*

I'd fine-tuned the criteria to go burgling to such a degree that 99.9 per cent of the time I always found something worth robbing once inside. Sometimes I ummed and ahh'd over stuff, but most times I knew what I was after and how much stuff was worth. After getting in and sorting out my escape route, my next move was to head straight for the dressing table in the main bedroom. This is where most people kept their jewels. I had a good eye. I knew my gold. European and English. The hallmarks on European gold weren't as clear as English marks, but the gold content was always richer, 14 carats, rather than English, which was 8 or 9. I took chains and stones, silver and gold, watches, clocks and money. Handfuls of money. Sovereigns, the older the better, pre-1960's sovereigns, I was told, weighing in at 22 carats instead of 18. I looked out for carriage clocks, specifically French and British, pre-1900s with repeaters and wind-ups. A carriage clock could be worth seven hundred quid or more. On one afternoon, rather than go home empty-handed, I took a grandfather clock to pieces and carried it out in bits. Painted grandfathers were worth more than non-painted, as were those with sun and moon dials on. Another time, I found a handgun under a bed and I wasn't quite sure whether to take it or not. I decided to shoot into a pillow to see and hear the effect of it, but then caution reined me in, and at the last moment I put the gun back under the bed where I'd found it.

Up until I was thirteen, I had to rely on my brothers to get my career off the ground. I used Martin to drive me to and from my burglaries and my brother Stephen to sell my haul afterwards. My profits were therefore a lot less than they might have been. What I really wanted and needed was my own car and my own *fences* to sell on to. Only then could I hope to make serious money.

***

It was a typical Monday morning. I left the house pretending to go to school and called for Bad Steve. I left my crutches and girdle in his bedroom and then we left his house pretending to go to school. We walked over to Peverell where the people with money lived, about a mile or two away from Swilly. There's no doubt I could have got shut of my girdle a lot sooner had I kept it on all the time, but that would have meant no burgling at all.

We picked a terrace of big houses and set to, knocking on doors, watching, counting. We counted the chimneys of the houses that were empty then went round the back and counted the chimneys again, so we burgled the right house, the empty house. This was a typical school day for us. On a Monday we always felt energetic. We wanted money for bus fares and sweets and Devon Hills (cider), and, if we were lucky, clothes, or at least, by the end of the week, a slap-up meal in the *Steak and Omelette*.

We weren't at school but we were learning geography, history, maths, economics and all in real time. We developed an instinctive grasp of what they now call an area's demographic profile. We knew our ABC1s from our no-hopers because we knew who was rich, who wasn't, and who was trying to be. By way of hallmarks and the features on antiques and effects, we learned the dates of battles, of dead kings and hung queens, and we accrued knowledge of craftsmen, guilds and the history of European metallurgy. By way of buying and selling, we learned about supply, demand, profit and loss, and enough maths to manage and broker multiple options and deals in our sleep. At school we felt thick, stupid and out of our depth. On the street, we felt very much at home – well, we were in lots of people's homes actually.

We went round the back, down the cobbled lane and climbed over the tall gate that got us into the backyard of chimney number five. I set to on the kitchen window with a screwdriver. The window frame was wood, old and I hoped rotting. I gouged away at it, in the gap, trying to force it open. It was hard. It wouldn't budge. We took it in turns. Then we heard sirens. We paused. We looked around. We'd been a bit daft. It was broad daylight. The backs of the houses on the next street over were bearing down on us. Some of the houses were three storeys high. There were at least fifty windows with a grandstand view of our attempt to break and enter. The sirens got louder. We knew they were for us.

We ran. We ran off the streets and into Central Park, taking the widest road that runs straight down the middle of it. We could see the coppers running into the park after us. We couldn't run any faster and they were gaining ground. We were out in the open and they were moving in on us from two different directions. There was at least half a dozen of them. We headed for the zoo. We saw the police running up the hill and down again, all in uniform with helmets on. We couldn't run any faster or any further – completely knackered. We decided to hide in the bushes at the entrance to the zoo. From our hiding place we could see them all spreading out, looking for us. We were still out of breath and in stitches, laughing. Then one of them nabbed us from behind.

They took us down to Charles Cross Police Station. My mother was called in to attend the interview. Because we didn't actually enter the house we were accused of burgling (not for want of trying) and because we forgot to ditch our screwdrivers after making our escape, we'd gone "equipped".

CHAPTER 4

REPORT TO PLYMOUTH JUVENILE COURT

11th June 1978

CONCERNING: David James Hill D.O.B: 19.9.64

ADDRESS: 91, Grassendale Avenue, North Prospect, Plymouth.

OFFENCES: Theft (three cases).

PREVIOUS: Burglary – no further action taken because of age. Theft – Plymouth Juvenile Court 20.4.77 – two-year supervision order

FAMILY:
Father   Deceased
Mother   Rosalie Mary Hill – housewife
Siblings: Stephen Hill, Martin Hill, Anthony Hill, Maureen Hill, David James Hill

---

Home: This family took up residence at their present home, etc.
Father: Mr Hill died nearly three years ago (sic) of thrombosis. He originated, etc.
Mother: Mrs Hill is a housewife. She was born in the South Hams and lived in Bristol, etc.

Concerned:

David is the youngest in the family. The family have had their troubles in the past. David attended the Pennycross Primary School, etc. He attends no youth club, preferring to use his spare time for fishing or riding his bicycle.

Offences:

This is not the first time David has come to the notice of the police. On 21st July 1974 David was involved in a burglary but no further action was taken as at the time as he was under the age of criminal responsibility. On 20th April 1977, he was made the subject of a supervision order for two years at the Plymouth Juvenile Court, for theft. He has been constantly reminded to keep out of trouble, unfortunately at the moment to no avail. However, he has expressed his regret for the offences for which he now appears before this court.

Conclusion:

It is regrettable that David seems to be following the example of his older brothers in the field of criminal activity. He will not be fourteen years of age until 19th September 1978, and Your Worships may feel that the time is now opportune to make David realise that he cannot commit criminal offences with impunity...

Signed: Mr A. Briggs, Social Worker
Devon County Council Social Services Department

***

Greg Cook the social worker came to see me. He was wearing an impressive beard and driving a yellow Citroen 2CV. His job was to find the best course of action to stop the rot and convert me from a juvenile delinquent into a law-abiding youth with prospects. His sloping shoulders and his "No" to the offer of a cup of tea betrayed his pessimism as to the likely success of this, his latest adventure into Swilly.

Since I'd already run out of cautions, and because I was related to (and living on the same street as) some of the most prolific thieves in the city, Greg felt that a custodial sentence was inevitable.

I think Mum was embarrassed by my behaviour. It was only when some official showed up that we became fully aware of how we must appear to others. And at those times a twinge of guilt did run through me, but only a twinge, to be honest. I think Mum felt all the guilt we didn't. To justify what appeared to be her sons' blatant disregard for the law and for society in general, she tried to paint a picture that Greg the social worker could empathise with. This was a good time to wheel out the dead dad story. I have never used my dead dad to justify my bad behaviour because I can't. I didn't and don't believe it, but perhaps

Mum did, just a little.

"And how old was David when his father died?"

"I was five. I *am* still here you know."

"And since then you've been a right little tearaway?" He crossed his legs and sucked his pen.

I didn't answer.

"So it's all your dad's fault is it?" He sat forward to get me to speak. I didn't have much respect for grown men driving yellow cars, especially Citroen 2CVs. I couldn't take him seriously.

"Well 'ardly. He's dead. Weren't you listenin'?"

"But if he wasn't dead, if he was still here, perhaps your life... and your brothers'... well perhaps things might have turned out differently?"

"I s'pose so. He'd 'ave battered us. Or we'd've battered 'im. S'ard to say, I never really knew the man."

"You never married again, Mrs Hill?"

Talking to kids about their dead dad was a skill he hadn't yet got to grips with.

"No. I'm still on my own." This was a lie.

"They say families can survive without fathers, but you know, in my job, you'd be forgiven for thinking that was something of a myth. It can't have been easy for you, Mrs Hill. But still, I must ask you what steps can you take to stop this one going the same way as his brothers? You've got two in borstal already, I'm told?"

I got up as if to leave, and perfectly timed, I reached for my crutches.

"They're *your* crutches, are they? I *was* wondering. You been fightin' 'ave you, boy?"

"He's disabled, Mr Cook."

"Is he? What's wrong with him? Is he registered disabled with the court?" He checked his notes to see if any disability had been recorded. "Disabled? It says here he gave the police a bloody good run for their money?"

"Well he's getting better now. But he's been disabled all his childhood pretty much. Show 'im your girdle, David."

I lifted my T-shirt so he could see the now well-worn dirty pink girdle that encased my torso. And that's when Greg the social worker with a dose of optimism entered the room. It was all change.

"What's wrong with you, lad?" he said, with a deep tone of sympathy, sombre like.

"I've got Perthes' disease."

"Perthes' disease?" He was writing furiously in his notebook, not letting on that he had no idea what Perthes' disease was. He looked up, expectantly, from me to my mother and back to me again.

I gave him chapter and verse on the nature of my condition as I understood it. I explained how it had interrupted my schooling. I milked it. He was impressed with my understanding of the hip bone and how much I knew about the nature of the treatment I'd endured.

"Well, I guess that explains why you might feel a bit... "different" to all the other lads. And I expect having brothers who've already gone off the rails... well, I suppose there hasn't been much in the way of incentive to buckle down, has there? Unfortunate really, because you're a bright lad, I can see that."

"It's been hard for *me* as well you know," said Mum, feeling the blame arrow swinging back round to her again. "I've tried my best with *all* of them."

"Well, Mrs Hill, before coming here, I was quite happy to go along with the standard recommendation of a long spell in a detention centre. This would have been a fit punishment for David, given his history to date. I was of the opinion that he needs a short sharp shock to truly understand that a life of crime is neither lucrative nor pleasant. But given what you've just told me... thank you, David, I wonder if we shouldn't take a more psychological approach to his situation. Perhaps we could encourage your son to explore his inner world in a bit more depth rather than put him through the rigour of the physical challenge and raw discipline he'd be in for at a detention centre. In truth, I think I'd like to avoid the risk of his physical health deteriorating any further. I can't promise anything, but that would be my recommendation. They don't always listen to us social workers. They think we're a soft touch."

Again, with his pen poised at the ready and my file opened out across his knee, he looked up and asked me, "David, given a clean ticket, a clean bill of health, and a chance to start over again, how do you see your future shaping out?"

I trotted out the usual rubbish. I told him I was planning to get a job in the dockyard, that I wanted to grow up and have a family and a decent house to live in, to go on holiday abroad and all the rest of it. I played the game, not to distract or deceive, but for want of anything more concrete to tell him. What else could I say? That I was bent on a life of crime because it's what I enjoyed most and, more importantly, what I was good at?

It was about a week later when my doctor took off his half-moon specs and told me that I wouldn't be needing my crutches any more. The ball and socket of my hip bone were working perfectly together. I was as good as new. Cured. I could put all my weight on both legs without risking permanent disability. I'd already figured this out, of course, but it was good to hear it officially from a doctor. I didn't much fancy marching across parade grounds on crutches.

General Report – 13.6.78

David appeared at Plymouth Juvenile Court today on three offences of theft/burglary. There was a "finding of guilt" on each and the magistrate imposed a twelve-hour attendance centre order in respect of each offence. He was again reminded of the real need to keep out of trouble.

***

School

I suppose I ought to give some mention to school before continuing with my recollections.

The "learn your way out of poverty" plan didn't hold much merit for me. I didn't have any kind of track record for academic study and felt no inclination or aspiration to get one. My home tutors, who turned up twice a week to see how little work I'd done, took time out to explain how damaging it would be to my future prospects if I didn't "mark their words", "take the bull by the horns", "wake up", "knuckle down", "listen carefully" and "learn". Having a teacher all to myself meant I suffered rather more of these pep talks than your average Swilly lad. By the tender age of ten I'd learned the only sensible option for me would be to play to my strengths.

Big school wasn't much of an improvement on primary school. There was little to be had in the way of entertainment for a boy with more interest in hallmarks than exam marks. I did sometimes end up in a lesson or at a dance inadvertently if I was avoiding somebody or it was raining, but I tried hard not to. I did burglaries. Sometimes I'd take a day off and jump on a bus to Tavistock just for the hell of it, with a bag full of sweets to munch on.

I only ever went to school if Bad Steve went too, and then we'd spend the day searching for stuff to rob. We didn't steal from the kids (they didn't have anything). We went after unattended handbags, cash boxes and unlocked desk drawers. We regularly robbed the school tuck box of both cash and stock, and we'd climb up into the skylights above the art room to take our haul up onto the roof, where, without fear of interruption, we could eat the proceeds at our leisure in the sunshine.

I did on occasion show some flashes of brilliance that, in hindsight, *could* be read as signs of untapped merit. I've always been good with my hands, and for a short while at least, I excelled at woodwork and metalwork. The school's drive for efficiency forced them to teach us both woodwork and metalwork in one combined session. This was the only *"roll-up-your-sleeves-and-do-something-with-your-hands-lads"* session on offer to us, and after football, it was by far the most popular event of the week, especially for boys deemed "less academic" (most of us).

The teacher was dead chuffed with me, because for a short spell at least, I did turn up to his lessons and got on with my work whilst I was in them. We were tasked to make a piece of metal jewellery from a mould. I worked on a template for a metal brooch. I crafted my mould using the exact shape and pattern of a fifty pence piece. The teacher (who spent most of his time ensuring we didn't kill each other) viewed my "coin" brooch as a good example of a modern innovative design. I cracked on. Every week I came back to class to perfect my art, churning out as many metal brooches as I could in the time allowed. Then I hired young children to transform them into legal tender at the local sweet shop, their instructions to spend no more than a shilling at a time. The scam was scuttled when the shopkeeper dropped one of the coins on the floor – the noise it made gave the game away. Not a bad effort though, really.

Ordinarily limited in my ability to demonstrate my capacity for resourcefulness, invention and ingenuity, these lessons afforded me a chance to show a *flash* of brilliance that ought to have been recognised as a sign of my potential. I recognised it, so why couldn't they?

They say that everyone has a special teacher – the "one" who made a difference. Well, I remember mine being Brian the English teacher. He used to bring his guitar into class and sing to us. I think he enjoyed our classes the most as well. One day we found out that he'd broken his guitar and couldn't play it any more. I offered to buy him a new one. He didn't take me seriously at first but I persisted. There was something... I don't know... I just liked it when he played. On the rare occasions when I was there to listen to him, I felt like I'd been ripped off if he didn't play. When I asked him where I could go to buy one, he got a bit concerned. Only then did he realise I wasn't kidding. I was only about twelve. He warned me off. I remember feeling a bit hurt by this reaction. It wasn't like I was a naturally generous person. I never bought my mother bugger all. Oh, and there was another teacher who I quite liked – Frank. He taught history, I think. I remember wielding a couple of chairs and chasing him around the classroom with them. He did at least have a laugh with us. For any teachers out there, having a good laugh can make all the difference.

Bad Steve could hold a pen to the page with a lot more authority than me. I've always found it difficult to read and write, and my spelling was and still is atrocious. I hated being so slow and so incapable and I hated that I was judged on my performance with a pen. To compensate and to distract, I was generous with both my charm and humility, whereas Bad Steve, who didn't feel at all vulnerable or a need to defend himself, expressed his confidence with an excessive use of bad language. He breathed obscenities. He was vulgar, crude, and, even for me, a bit embarrassing sometimes. Unsurprisingly, the teachers didn't take to him. His contributions to the class effort were invariably either ignored or the cause of great upset. Suffice to say, neither of us ever felt very welcome at school. And so we left without any qualifications. None whatsoever.

So that was school then. All done.

***

Mum

My mum was a beautiful woman and a young widow. She spent her energies keeping her boys fed and watered. She made our beds, daily. Week in, week out, she laboured, washing, ironing, fetching and carrying. She was devoted to us. She'd have preferred to get the painters and decorators in before putting her sons through the bother of lifting a finger to help her. To the outside world, this was a normal house, complete with farmyard wallpaper in the kitchen, bottles of milk on the doorstep and bills all paid.

None of us helped her worry about the bills or pay them, in case you were interested. She didn't ask us to. She would have spent her last penny feeding us, and after that she'd turn to the local loan shark, before giving up or giving in. He came round collecting regularly, in a suit and tie and nice as pie. He'd let Mum borrow as much as she dared because she always paid him back. My mum would sit him down in the kitchen and give him cups of tea like he was a visiting dignitary.

A chance to love again did come her way. She started dating a man called Jim, who worked for the electricity board as a dredger. I say dating. I don't know if he ever took her anywhere. He was round the house a lot, that's what I noticed. He seemed OK. No bother to me. I only really noticed him at all because he collected old bottles that he dredged up from the bottom of the rivers he was working on. These bottles started appearing on the mantlepiece and windowsills as permanent fixtures. So we knew changes were afoot.

Our Stephen wasn't happy about it. Being the eldest, he'd enjoyed a long stint of playing *man about the house*, albeit he was hardly ever in the house or even in the country by the time Mum came clean about the true nature of this new "friendship", as she liked to call it. I think Stephen was in jail when Jim finally came clean, so it can't have been easy for Stephen to come home to find some bloke's got his feet under his table. Can't have been easy for Jim either.

Stephen didn't bother with the small talk – he made his feelings clear straight away. He never spoke to Jim at all. Not directly. Whilst Stephen had trouble looking people in the eye, he couldn't even look at Jim when they were in the same room together. If and when they did confront one another, it was always a Mexican stand-off. Stephen held off from creating any real friction or generating a rationale for violent conflict because he didn't want to spoil things for Mum. None of us did.

She seemed a lot happier *with* Jim than without him. For two whole years, give or take a few intervals courtesy of Her Majesty, Stephen managed to avoid hurting him. And when he was locked up, Jim dredged his way through Mum's domestic arrangements, picking and choosing what he would and wouldn't put up with.

Mum began to wear her hair in different styles, and she laughed and sang as she cooked and cleaned. She had a grown-up for company of an evening and she liked to make a ceremony of it, fluffing up the cushions and getting biscuits in. It had never occurred to me that she even *might* have been sad or lonely. Only after seeing a man take some interest in her did I realise that I never had. So I was kind-ish to Jim. I didn't give him grief. When I came home to find Mum singing in the kitchen, I felt a warm glow of satisfaction. Who wouldn't want that?

***

Statutory Visit Report: 7.2.80

Visited the Hill household following request regarding David's involvement with a burglary charge. Mrs Hill was at work. She returns approximately 5 pm each evening. I spoke to David for approximately forty-five minutes and he appears to be an inarticulate boy who cannot give any definitive statements about his involvement in the burglary incident. I explained the seriousness of his position based upon his previous criminal record. David reacts in a negative way to the consequence of his actions. He does not present himself as aggressive or of a dominant personality.

Statutory Visit Report: 8.2.80 5 pm

Visited again and spoke to Mrs Hill and David. She is a thin-faced anxious-looking woman and stated that she could not understand why David acted as he did.

Suggested she contact a solicitor, Stephen Walker, but she in fact contacted Mr. Goldberg. She has no real idea of what was best for David and felt that he was being led by others. (Trimm?)

Statutory Visit Report: 14.2.80

Visited and spoke to Mrs. Hill and David. Mrs. Hill seems rather unrealistic about David's behaviour. She states that David will change. David is also saying he has learned his lesson, but both these points are debatable. I pointed out quite strongly that David is using up his chances of staying out of the custodial network. Discussed the possibilities open to us regarding David's court appearance.

Statutory Visit Report: 2.4.80

Following the departure of Mr. Blackburn, I took over the responsibility for David and the presentation of the Court Report today. I have been in contact with Neathern Brock IT Centre and unfortunately, they are unable to offer David a place until their September intake. Despite this, I have not altered the Court Report asking for a deferred sentence.

At court today, David's solicitor (Goldberg) did not appear but had asked for an adjournment in the absence, which they were granted.

STILL SMALL VOICE

REPORT TO PLYMOUTH JUVENILE COURT

2nd April 1980

CONCERNING: David James Hill

D.O.B: 19.9.64

ADDRESS: 91, Grassendale Avenue, North Prospect, Plymouth.

OFFENCES: Joint burglary with intent.

PREVIOUS: Burglary – no further action taken because of age.

20.4.77 – Theft – Plymouth Juvenile Court – two-year supervision order

13.6.79 – Theft – attendance centre twelve hours with £32.52 compensation.

Father	Deceased
Mother	Rosalie Mary Hill – housewife
Siblings:	Stephen Hill
	Martin Hill
	Anthony Hill
	Maureen Hill
Concerned:	David James Hill

Home:

The family occupy a three-bedroomed house on a council estate noted for its high degree of delinquency. The property is maintained to a high standard of decoration and furnishing.

Father:

Mr Hill died nearly six years ago of thrombosis. (sic)

Mother:

Mrs Hill presents herself as a concerned but somewhat overburdened mother who has had to carry the full responsibilities of a large growing family during their formative adolescent years. Her two eldest sons have extensive criminal records. Mrs Hill is very concerned that David does not follow in their footsteps. However, she appears to be unable to take any positive action to prevent this happening. Mrs Hill now works full-time.

Concerned:

David was made the subject of two-year supervision order by the local authority at the Plymouth Juvenile Court on 20th April 1977. During this period, he offended again and was required to comply with an attendance centre order for 12 hours and pay compensation of £32.50. David's school record leaves much to be desired regarding timekeeping and attendance and he appears to lack motivation and commitment to his education and future job prospects. David does express interest in physical activities such as running, and he has at the moment a steady girlfriend. These activities do, according to his mother, occupy most of his spare time.

However, David's continuing contact with members of his peer group has an obvious bearing upon his involvement in criminal activities. He presents himself as an inarticulate sensitive youth with no indication of an aggressive attitude and with little or no control over the pattern of his life. Therefore, likely to respond to some form of structured programme which attempts to give guidelines and choices for his future. Any specific punitive sentence on David is likely to give him kudos amongst his peers and within his family and to have no long-term benefits, either for the youth or society.

Offence:

David fully admits that he was found in a suspicious manner but states that no specific act of theft was committed at the time. He is unable to articulate satisfactorily the reason for his actions. He has received several cautions in the past for similar incidents.

Conclusion:

David is aware that he may be deprived of his liberty. However, if this were to happen on a purely punitive basis, I feel it would be detrimental to the long-term interests of this boy and will only serve to reinforce any negative criminal attitudes he already holds. His family background, of which the lack of a stable male figure during his formative years of adolescence and his brothers' present position, is particularly worth noting, and has given David little opportunity to consider his pattern of behaviour.

Following discussion with Neathern Brock Intermediate Treatment Centre, Tavistock, Plymouth, it is felt that David would benefit from the structured environment which it provides.

To allow positive work to be done on this youth, I would respectfully suggest to Your Worships that he receive a deferred sentence so that a place at Neathern Brock could be taken up, while not removing from David the possibility of punitive action being taken by the court should he re-offend during the order.

Such a course of action would give David a final chance before he embarks upon the path his brothers have taken.

Signed: Miss Corith Jones, Social Worker

Devon County Council

Social Services Department

Statutory Visit Report: 14.4.80

Informed by my colleague Mr Heath that when he was on day duty on Friday the 11th, he was called to the police station to sit in on an interview with David, who was accused of burglary. According to Mr Heath, there was an eyewitness who identified David. David denied the offence.

Statutory Visit Report: 21.4.80

Visited David and Mrs Hill at home. I feel very sorry for Mrs Hill as she has put all her efforts into producing a family of villains and she simply doesn't have any control over their activities. Her attitude is that she has told David off and he has promised he won't do anything wrong again, therefore David won't re-offend. David denied that he was involved in the burglary on 11.4.80. As it stands at the moment, there are three offences to be dealt with.

(1) Burglary with intent (1 case)

(2) Discharge of a firearm (1 case)

(3) TDA

In the light of the lack of the place at Neathern Brock until September 1980, I have rewritten the Court Report, altering the recommendation from a deferred sentence (I do not think the court would entertain this as a place is not available until September) to asking for a supervision order with the normal three requirements.

Statutory Visit Report: 16.6.80

I visited last week but David was not at home. Mike Mogridge (EWO) had rung to discuss David's lack of school attendance since approx. March. He has tried on numerous occasions to discuss the situation with Mrs Hill. However, he has not succeeded. He now feels that as there has been no improvement it would be appropriate to take Mrs Hill to court. I explained that we had only recently obtained a supervision order and that I hadn't yet visited. Mike agreed to give me a couple of weeks' grace to see if I could work any miracles. Apparently, David's absences coincide with those of his erstwhile partner in crime Stephen T.

***

I was kind to Jim, but only so long as he didn't mess with my head, so long as he didn't get to thinking he could "be my dad". Maureen, me and Jim were sitting at the table waiting for Mum to bring the dinner in. All my brothers were out. The police had been round to ask questions about some local robbery I wasn't involved in but our Tony had been. Then Mum came in with the dinner.

"You know," Jim said, "if they had to pay rent, they might treat you with a bit more respect here?"

I glared long enough to let Jim know he was chancing his arm. Did he not know that Mum would always put us first, not him?

"Can I go an' watch telly, Mum?"

"Yes, son."

"No. You sit at the table and eat," said Jim.

I turned the TV up really loud. It was the Fonz, *Happy Days*.

I never spoke to him again after that. Not a word.

He didn't propose to my mother, but he did ask her to move up to

Liverpool with him, generously offering to take me and Maureen as well but leaving behind all my brothers. He clearly *didn't* know my mother well enough.

And that was the end of Jim.

No more Mum singing in the kitchen.

STILL SMALL VOICE

CHAPTER 5

Take Your Pick...

The judge gave me a choice: eight weeks of a SHORT SHARP SHOCK regime in a detention centre (DC) – a boot camp complete with fists and knobs on – or six weeks in Neathern Brock, an American-inspired "Intermediate Treatment Centre" for the rehabilitation of youth offenders. In Neathern Brock I'd be shacked up in a big house in the countryside with another twenty kids who'd also gone off the rails. By agreeing to undergo "Intermediate Treatment", my mother gave the authorities permission to mess with my head. The Neathern Brock programme was designed by well-meaning shrinks who believed in revolutionary techniques to bring about a fundamental psychological shift in the most hardened of juvenile delinquents.

It was my choice and it wasn't difficult. I'd already endured a number of days of punishment in Plymouth's attendance centre. It was a punishment centre. You were sent there to endure some of the more insidious aspects of the treatment meted out to boys in a DC – but you could go home at night, so it was just a taster really, a deterrent. You could go on any day of the year and any number of times, but the regime was identical, as were the men who ran it, all in uniforms, marching around, waving sticks about and shouting orders through cartoon moustaches under peaked caps. On the deterrent measure, they hit the spot. I had no wish to experience the full-fat version in a DC. Undergoing a psychological shift in a country house sounded a lot more cushy.

***

11.7.80 – **Home visit**

Seen David Hill and Mrs Hill.

Following discussions with social worker, it was decided that the initial visit would be devoted to explaining NB to David and his mother and that if David's reaction was favourable then a further interview would be arranged.

The Hills live in a comfortably furnished local authority house in North Prospect, Plymouth. David presents as a tall slim-looking boy with quite long hair and a very engaging manner. His dress is flamboyant, and on this occasion he was wearing skin-tight jeans and a collarless shirt with puff sleeves.

Both Mrs Hill and David listened to my talk about NB and appeared to understand the aims and objectives. Both David and his mother appeared receptive to David's going there, and a second visit was arranged for Tuesday, 15th July.

11.7.80 – School Visit

Saw Mr C, the headmaster. Mr C stated that David's attendance had improved greatly since the institution of the supervision order but he still tends to arrive late and leave at will. He doesn't present any management problem when he is actually within the school. Mr C stated that on numerous occasions David had been known to spend quite large sums of money with one of his friends, Steve T (this is no relative of Andrew T). Despite the way in which David likes to spend money, he apparently does not have respect for it.

On one occasion a member of staff had seen him and Stephen T in town talking to a known homosexual, and it is *felt that in view of his physical presentation, it may prove positive to look further into David's sexual orientation.*

David is of average intelligence but is under-achieving.

Mr C felt that there was room for hope in David due to his recently improved behaviour, and felt that his main problem lay in his lack of self-esteem.

15.7.80 Home Visit

Saw David and his mother. Mrs Hill described David as being very helpful around the house and felt that she was able to tell him off with some effect. She saw him as being no real problem to herself and stated that she trusted him. She felt that he was not very communicative, but this appears to be an overall problem and not restricted to her.

David saw the most positive thing about himself as being the way that he dressed. On being pressed, he was also able to say that he thought he was kind. It was very difficult for him to say that he thought he was kind, but it was quite easy for him to be positive about his dress. The only bad point he could see about himself was that he was too small.

David says that he is very fond of his mother and his brother and enjoys living at home. He says that he helps out around the house quite often and said that if he was the first person home, then he would do the washing up or any other work without being asked.

He said that he didn't receive regular pocket money but knew that his mother would give him money when it was necessary. He seemed to accept the situation as being normal. David cites his interests as being fishing, badminton, pool, cricket, running and Motown recordings. He also said that he enjoyed cooking.

Induction interview at NB arranged for Tuesday 19th August at 6 pm.

David is a lad who could easily be possessed of a great deal of charm. He has a certain physical poise and the ability to maintain eye contact. I believe he is motivated to change since he does not wish to follow his brothers' careers, as the (sic) improved self-image and positive external support.

Fully clothed

It took almost a year before they finally carted me off to serve my time. During that time, I'd enjoyed some success, amassing £600 pounds sterling and a top of the range racing bike. On the morning of my leaving, I stashed the money in the attic and gave Bad Steve my precious bike to look after.

The judge, the police, the social worker, my mother and me – we all knew the truth. Removing me from home was really just an inconvenient and annoying interruption of operations for me. I was running a very lucrative enterprise. More broadly, I knew it would be a complete waste of time – both theirs and mine.

This was confirmed the minute I arrived at Neathern Brock. I knew straight off that I was the smartest kid in the building. The ones who *thought* they were smart were all vandals and would-be escapees – opening conversations were pretty much focussed on how to screw the screws over. These kids thought they were smart *because* they were bucking the system. I couldn't see the wisdom of risking yet more punishment and a longer sentence for crimes that weren't worth committing in the first place – defiling pictures, nicking cutlery, etc. I behaved myself – as well as I could – given the provocations. I showed no inclination to break the rules or break out of there. I wanted guaranteed freedom as soon as it could be delivered and no later. How could I become a successful burglar if I was a) on the run or b) banged up all the time?

Our *treatment* at Neathern Brock was designed to restructure and rebuild our identity, so we were told. They were going to "strip us down to build us up again". Still better than being made to run five miles, cross country, in your skiddies before breakfast every morning. We had beanbags to sit on at Neathern Brock. And carpets. And there were pictures on the walls in all the bedrooms.

Being stripped of their identity whilst clutching onto a beanbag was a little bit too traumatic for some. This "stripping" was in fact just a ritual humiliation. Each one of us took turns to be ridiculed, insulted, shamed and put down. The psychological warfare always took place in the Orange room. As you'd expect, floor to ceiling, this room was painted orange, and it was empty but for a heap of orange beanbags. Even the carpets and curtains were orange. And the cups.

"David, you are a thief. Everyone in your family is a thief. Your brothers are the scum of the earth. You are the scum of the earth."

This is a good example of the general tone and nature of their approach.

"Mary, stand up. Look at you. Look at the state of you. You are a slut. You've always been a slut and you always will be a slut. All the boys have been through you, you slut. Now sit down and stop it with those crocodile tears. SIT DOWN."

They put on these sessions every day, each one of us being hauled up in front of the others, to be shamed, to be made to feel worthless.

In the evenings, after dinner, it was all change. Now we had to congregate in the Green room. Here the staff fell over themselves to be kind to us. They gave us tea and cake and told us how marvellous we were and what great people we'd grow up to be, once we had a better understanding of who we were and what we were capable of. This bit of the treatment completed the head-fuck. I think they expected us to be so desperate to be saved, to belong, to be worth something, that with a bit of chivvying on their part, in the Green room, they could tip us over from not being bothered to desperately *"wanting"* to believe the best of ourselves. Compared to how awful we were, had been, could be, the Green room treatment positioned us as potential soldiers of industry. We would all grow up to have impeccable manners, be honest, hard-working and determined to make something of ourselves.

Thankfully they let us wear our own clothes all the time we were in there. Unlike most fourteen-year-olds at that time, clothes for me were hugely important. This was down to the fact that from an early age I'd always idolised our Martin for his fashion sense. He bought all his clothes from top tailors in town, and I followed suit when funds allowed. So whilst the Neathern Brock crew took great pains to strip away our identity, it's ironic they left me with my clothes on and my identity fully intact. I remember being very attached to a pair of tight pink velvet trousers which I wore with a generous flowing white shirt tucked in and puffed out. The staff would comment on my fashion sense, my body, my attractiveness. They were gay, I realise now. Sadly, I think they were perverts too. I don't know who they got at in there, or how many, but I was spared. I wouldn't have been an easy lay, and I think they might have just picked up on that and steered clear.

The other kids were labelled bad and/or mad, but the truth is none of them were even *that* interesting. Had they been madder and badder, I wouldn't have got quite so bored in there. Whilst the men doling out the treatment in this place were very good at "hollowing out" the mind of low-intellect serial offenders, what they didn't quite manage to do was to leave the most vulnerable with enough resilience to cope with the insidious and widespread bullying that went on once *their* "treatment" sessions were over. One lad was forced to carry a girl's rucksack around for her everywhere she went. He followed her about like a slave, doing whatever she told him to do. Stockholm syndrome ensued. He developed a crush on her. When she dumped him, he lost it and tried to drown himself.

I spent my fifteenth birthday in there: September, 1979. The lads tossed me into the air in a sheet which ripped, and so I fell straight through it and from a great height. I don't know if my Perthes' disease affected my rate of growth, but by fifteen I hadn't grown very tall. I still didn't look old enough to drive a car. Still, I was far wiser than most fifteen-year-olds, and a lot richer too.

***

I guess my family must have been a bit concerned. One day, our Martin turned up for a visit. He was driving a golden three-litre Ford Capri, unusual in its day and bought wholly with stolen money. I was more jealous than pleased to see him. His wealth, his suntan, his freedom, his casual cheek and laid-back boldness – it all intensified my desire to get out of there quickly. And so I did everything they said to the letter and immediately – not a sneer of rebellion could be read from my expression. Unlike the others, I never complained (out loud) about any of the treatment they subjected me to. After six weeks' imprisonment, I was at last discharged and free to go out robbing again.

Nothing had changed. Except that our Tony had gone and got himself a job in the Toshiba factory. None of us had ever had a job. Well except for Mum of course. She had three on the go.

***

R. Blackburn, Esq.,

Social Services,

Wolseley House

Wolseley Road,

Plymouth

Dear Roger,

Re: David James Hill

Enclosed please find two copies of the report on David after his month block at Neathern Brock. We have also sent a copy to Camel's Head school. We look forward to receiving more information about the burglary incident mentioned on the phone yesterday.

Yours sincerely,

Bruce De Walt

Project Director

Neathern Brock Report – 9th October 1980

DAVID JAMES HILL

BORN 19.9.64

AGED 15 YEARS

COURSE ATTENDED 8.9.80

REASONS FOR REFERRAL

David was placed on his second supervision order in April 1980, with an intermediate treatment requirement, as a result of being brought before the police several times for various offences of theft and burglary.

Not only is he resident in an area associated with a high degree of delinquent behaviour, his three older brothers have had a great involvement with the police and were felt to be having too strong an influence on David.

PEER GROUP RELATIONSHIPS

Initially, David seemed to find difficulty in realising that he was expected to participate in activities as a member of the group and not purely as an individual. A note in the occurrence book recorded after the camping trip reads: "David always wandering off ahead of the main group." The trip showed David to be impatient and restless. He had to be constantly reminded that he belonged to the group. However, David did form a relationship with one of the leading female members of the group, and initially this seemed to serve not only as an anchor, but as a way to establish a position for himself within the group.

As his confidence grew, David became the popular comic of the group; placed very centrally in all the special exercises. He developed a somewhat detached leadership, seeming to make little effort to develop or maintain ties, though he did form a very close relationship with another male resident, and was seen very much as the influential and leading member of this partnership.

David was invariably at the centre of all the practical joking, but he often seemed unable to restrain himself from carrying a joke too far.

First, he began to emerge as a somewhat untrustworthy member of the group. Intelligent and perceptive enough to realise the weak points of others, he used this information for material entertainment at their expense.

STAFF RELATIONSHIPS

David appeared to be quite at ease mixing with adults, and had a friendly and relaxed relationship with all the staff, also showing an ability to be mature, serious and intelligently enquiring, when not surrounded by his peer group audience.

ATTITUDE AND PROGRESS TO GROUP WORK AND COUNSELLING

Entrance in the occurrence notes on the second day of the intake reads "very giggly and seems to use this as an escape valve during group sessions". This comment could have been repeated many times during the month. His continued loud giggling and passing of witty, critical comments. He became very disruptive and allowed others to use his behaviour as an excuse for their own occasional lack of interest or concentration.

David gave the impression of being completely satisfied with himself and his own situation, and this was reflected in his very shallow contribution to group discussion and his disinterest in concentrating on any problem areas within himself or his family. Although he did find it very difficult and uncomfortable evaluating some things, he was quite perceptive of inadequacies in others and could be very harshly critical. His ability to confine these criticisms to an apparently humorous level allowed him to maintain his own popularity. He was not a resident who encouraged confidence in others in a group situation, and showed himself to be very unsupportive and, at times, was a very thoughtless and tactless member of the group

In a one-to-one counselling situation, David was relaxed and serious, able to converse willingly on a variety of subjects, but unforthcoming and apparently uninterested in pursuing any areas of his own life.

APTITUDES, ABILITIES, MOTIVATION AND INTERESTS

One of David's main interests seem to be clothes. He possesses an extensive fashionable wardrobe, which he was happy to share with the female residents, and would frequently refer to a planned shopping trip on his return.

He also expressed a desire to join the merchant navy and seems to have a realistic idea of the educational expectations involved. How far he would be able to meet these expectations is a matter of some concern. Although he impresses as being reasonably intelligent, his written work is very poor, and he put very little effort into his scrapbook whilst at Neathern Brock.

One of David's most noticeable abilities was his success at entertaining others. His perceptions of other residents gave rise to sharp and sometimes cruel mimicking of others.

HEALTH AND HYGIENE

David has an attractive bright open face and was always impeccably clean and very tidily and fashionably dressed. He often changes clothes two or three times a day and seems to have an abhorrence of the idea of body odour, to the extent of using a great deal of very powerful-smelling *deodorant.*

FAMILY CONTACT

David only wrote home once and expressed a dislike of letter writing. He received few letters from home, though on his birthday he received a large number of cards and the present of an expensive watch from his mother. He seemed offhand and slightly awkward with his mother on parents' afternoon, though he did say he was very pleased to see her. It seems that some members of his family were told he was on holiday, as became evident when his brother attempted to visit him.

CONCLUSIONS AND RECOMMENDATIONS

It became evident at the review that David is very powerfully influenced by his peer group and family. The main concern for David at the moment seems to be whether or not he can avoid further police involvement before his supervision order expires. It was felt that the strongest way of supporting him in this is to continually remind him that the end of school is very much a reality and to let him know that we are aware of his limitations. Therefore, we are no longer encouraging his entry into the merchant navy, but rather endeavouring to fuel his interest in physical labour.

David is at the moment involved in a programme of work experience at school, which means he is out every Friday working as a tyre fitter. Next term, he will be encouraged to continue this full-time, with a view to being taken on as a regular employee when he does leave school.

Prognosis for this lad is poor. We believe that the negative times which already exist within the family, i.e. involvement with his brothers who may be at risk of serious offending, are so strong that it is unlikely he will avoid becoming involved.

There is an initial joint visit arranged with Ian Robertson and Roger Blackburn for Wednesday, 5th November at 10 am, and further statutory visits will be arranged on this date.

National Children's Home – NCH

Neathern Brock Intermediate Treatment Centre

Kilworthy Road, Tavistock, Devon PL19 0JL

STILL SMALL VOICE

Project Director: Bruce De Walt

20th November 1980

***

Back on the street...

As a safety precaution, we burgled all the easy ones in one area (keys left in doors, open windows, churches, sparking[1])... and then moved on

---

[1] We went sparking, outside parks and playgrounds, anywhere you find posh people going off for a walk with their kids and dogs. At the entrance to parks, you find roads full of parked cars belonging to people who don't come from that area. They just "nip" in the park to give the dog an empty. It wasn't just parks we went to, but these types of places were favourite for sparking. We'd look through the car windows first, for tell-tale signs - you only need to see an inch worth of a handbag strap to know you've got a target. Then, after spying something worth having – a car radio that's easy to detach – we'd try the door, more often than not, locked. That's where the "sparking" came in. If you smash the ceramic end of a spark plug with a hammer, the ceramic splits and fragments. You can use a piece of the ceramic fragment as a missile to throw at car window. The glass – yes, that really strong car window glass – instantly shatters. You can throw a reasonably large stone at a car window and nothing much will happen, but a tiny fragment of spark plug ceramic will destroy it, instantly. Once the glass was shattered, we could remove the valuables fairly simply and quietly. We could get through three or four an hour on a good day, and very lucrative work it was too, if somewhat risky.

to the next. On my prized bicycle I soon exhausted much of what I considered to be our home territory (well-heeled Plymouth) and so it became necessary to employ my older brother Martin as a driver to work the manors (and many were just that – manors) further afield. In many respects, our Martin was the ideal driver, in that he lacked any ambition to lead even though he was four years older than me. His long-term plan was always his current plan. "David! I've found the number to end all numbers." This was his cry when he came up with a decent target worth robbing. Every one of Martin's numbers was the one to *end all numbers*. I learned early on the limit of his potential (long before he did), but unlike the school teachers, I gave him credit for and scope to put his talents to some use, to earn a living from them. He was a half-decent driver, if a bit on the careful side.

For a long time, Martin was involved in transporting vanloads of electrical goods from the storerooms of Comet, Dixons and SWEB over to Ricky and Ron's, twin brothers who had their own little electrical shop. Ricky and Ron were early adopters, in actual fact. They launched one of the first video rental services in Plymouth. I went with our Martin on a couple of robberies that were used to replenish their stock. These robberies were a cinch compared to houses, so long as the research had been done correctly. No one cares about businesses getting hit, so you feel less on offer when you're emptying a place out. For Martin, these jobs were the number to end all numbers. Some of these businesses didn't even fit alarms on their premises back then, and their storerooms were always chocka. As for emptying them out quickly and efficiently, I think our Martin worked harder and smarter than any fully paid-up dedicated employee ever would. He took as much as he could carry from branches all over the region. He worked unsociable hours and without fear for his health and safety. He'd drive straight to Ricky and Ron's and back the van up to their storeroom ready for unloading. And then he'd unload without stopping even for a cup of tea. Afterwards, he'd go into the shop proper and hire a video off them, like it was the most normal thing in the world to do, heist over. He paid full price for it too. And back then, even we burglars were struggling to come down on one side or the other... Betamax or VHS?

Martin never turned down the chance to earn some money if he could be of help to someone else. He loved cars, and from him (and our Tony) I learned to love cars too. I knew when my time came, I'd drive a lot faster than him, better than him, and I'd make sure to always have better cars at my disposal than him. Until such times though, I was forced to rely on him to help me expand my operations geographically.

Having outstayed my welcome in Plymouth and exhausted what low-hanging fruit there was, access to a car came as a godsend. There were plenty of rich pickings in Noss Mayo, Tavistock, Exeter, Newton Ferrers. Cornwall. North Devon. We burgled all kinds of houses, big, small, rural, city. I pushed myself to the limit, robbing whoever, whenever, and I sold all my ill-gotten gains to my brothers, who sold them on to proper fences, who in turn sold them on to dealers up the line so ensuring any family heirlooms belonging to my victims didn't turn up in local shops where they could easily be traced back to the criminal families most likely to be responsible – ours being chief amongst them.

I dressed well. I ate well. I had stashes of cash and hot jewellery secreted all over the house, in the attic, embedded in floors and windowsills, in other people's houses. I was on fire.

I soon became impatient and unsatisfied with the level of service my brothers delivered when disposing of my assets. A couple of words in a couple of ears brought me into direct contact with a man called Keith Brown, a notorious fence who is now dead. He was a bit of a *geezer,* an antique-dealing landlord with multiple properties, very long hair, dubious morals and a fake cockney accent. Having my own fence meant my margins became a lot bigger and so did my incentive to burgle even more houses, every single day. For a fifteen-year-old lad, this was as good an introduction to the world of work as one could wish for.

"How about Cornwall for a change?"

Me and Martin. We were sitting outside our house, in the car, engine running but no strategy in place, no target to head for. Financially, I was ahead of myself, out in front, but that didn't mean I was any less motivated. Every day I perfected and practised my craft as dutifully as any artist, grasping every opportunity that came my way, with both hands, religiously.

"Whereabouts in Cornwall?"

"Where's that place, where the pirates 'ung out?"

"That would be all over."

"Someone wrote a book about it. A pub."

"*Jamaica Inn*?"

"Where's that?"

"Dunno."

"Just drive. Let's go an' find it."

Martin went with the flow, especially since he was guaranteed a payday nine times out of ten. I had the energy, the entrepreneurial spirit, the discipline. He had the wherewithal and the willingness to please when he was needed.

We forgot about *Jamaica Inn* and settled on a bungalow near Padstow instead. Martin parked the car up the road and I donned my Chinese slippers before slinking round the back of the building where I found some French doors to prise open.

It was an old woman's house. Lots of lace and silver. Candlesticks are a dead giveaway. Wedding photo on the bureau, black and white, costumes like they had in the war. She had miniature pieces of furniture crafted from mahogany, arranged on the sideboard as a kind of entertainment – some miniature people would have brought the idea to life. Sideboard drawers full of silver. I took the teaspoons. They looked special. This woman was special. Proper old school.

I liked bungalows. They were quick. No risk of being trapped upstairs.

In her bedroom, I gagged on the smell of Vicks and cats and headed straight for her jewellery box. In it, a spray of cheapish-looking pearls, which I took, and some rings, a ruby, a diamond, some costume stuff. I lifted the bed mattress expecting to find it clean but instead found a velvet pouch full of something hard. Huge diamonds. Whoppers. Four carats each. It was a haul to take your breath away.

I found some cash, more silver and some gold chains in the study. Then I got out.

We drove straight to Plymouth to see Keith Brown. We went to three different houses before we pinned him down at a large five-storey house he'd just bought close to the city centre. I went in on my own. He was busy, he said, preparing to rent the property out to students, stripping out all the architecturally valuable fixtures and fittings and replacing them with shite. He was young for a rich man and very focussed on his money-making ventures, as I was. I respected him. I had every intention of becoming a lot richer than him and a lot sooner.

As soon as he saw me at the door, he started fiddling round in his pocket for his glass. He took me down the hall and into a makeshift workshop he'd set up for his workmen to use. He found his bag and brought out his scales.

"'Ad 'elluva job findin' yer. Yer all over the place these days, aren't yer?"

"Don't stand still. That's my motto. What you got for me then, boy? S'gettin' to be a bit regular this, innit?"

I was, by some distance, his youngest supplier. I took the blue velvet bag from my jeans and pulled the drawstring. I didn't want to hand the diamonds over to him – I wanted to present them to him.

"P'raps we could set up a regular meetin' time so I don't 'ave to be chasin' you about all over town?"

He didn't show or let me know if he was contemplating this piece of advice. He worked quietly. He put all the lights on and then reached into a cupboard to pull out a desk lamp which was covered in dust. He blew on it and I just managed to dodge out the way. He lit the lamp, and then in front of it he laid down a piece of black velvet cloth across the workbench.

"I don't do owt reg'lar. Not safe in my game. Don't want people knowin' where I am all the time. Well come on then, boy, let's 'ave it then."

He rolled his eyeglass between his hands as if he were warming himself up whilst I rolled the diamonds onto his cloth, making sure they landed bang on, in the spotlight. The sparkle told the full story. Again, the diamonds took my breath away. Keith stayed silent. He was impressed.

He picked up a stone and turned it and turned it and then turned it again. Then he put it back and picked another. And again, until he'd gone through them all three times. I said nothing. I knew to stay cool. After a long time, he said, "Let's call it five grand, shall we?"

I now know those stones were worth fifty grand, minimum.

I only hope the old lady was insured.

***

Silver linings

Whilst it was useful having Martin to drive me around, I figured I could expand upon my position and potential by working solo as well, so I didn't give up on my "burgling by bike" exploits. I had two good legs now. Why not? I bought two new bikes from *Devon Bikes* and took to racing round posh estates, recce-ing, with Bad Steve. This was a good move. We got stuck in and a lot done. We sailed a bit too close to the wind, in fact, sticking to one particularly rewarding area for far too long. We became conspicuous, but I'd been too high on my newfound freedom to pay attention to this lapse in security.

On one of these adventures we went off the trail and down the drive of a large country manor house that looked *very* promising. An empty gravel car park in front of a double-fronted eaves-heavy house with leaded windows. Through the letter box and the glass doors of the inner porch I could see a series of hefty columns either side of the hallway, a wide spiral staircase and a minstrel's gallery. Round the back they had a croquet lawn and a large garden with a maze in the middle. They had dosh. I rang the front doorbell and waited long enough to figure the place was empty, but at the very last moment, just before we got stuck in, an old man answered the door.

"Can we 'ave a glass o' water, mister, please. I think I'm gonna faint."

He didn't fall for it. He came out into the front drive with us. He seemed to be looking for something behind us. He asked how we'd found the place. He knew what we were up to. We backed off. He followed us down the drive and watched us cycle off. We watched him shut the gate after us. He got a really good look at us.

We did pretty well, all told mind. After emptying a local church of its candlesticks and chalices, we accumulated enough silver to make a visit to Hatton Garden worthwhile. We made the papers too – *"Boys on bikes commit spate of robberies in Plymstock – beware!"*

Whilst silver doesn't sell for as much as gold, it's still a profitable, albeit problematic, commodity, needing a bit more care and attention so far as disposal is concerned. I never, or hardly ever, sold silver to fences, not without melting it down first, and only then if I was desperate for instant cash. That was rare, though. I usually had enough to tide me over. Silver was a saver – to be managed as an asset to be liquidated as and when I felt the need to, and the time was right.

I used to liquidate my silver assets in our back kitchen when Mum was at work. Melting silver was the most profitable and sensible way of solving what I called the "silver" problem. Gold is so much easier to sell.

Mass market gold chains and rings are universally indistinguishable from one another and fetch good money in quantity. Gold is worth its weight, as they say. Not so silver. Stolen silver "pieces" – unique bits of jewellery that are worth a bit more than their weight but not much more – are dangerous objects to be found in possession of. So the trick is to get as much silver together as you can and dispose of it all in one go. The problem with silver is its traceability. More often than not, silver jewellery is crafted by artists who are determined to leave their footprints all over it. As a result, you never get two pieces of "real" silver the same, and if you're nicked with any of it, the pieces they find on you will easily and inevitably get traced right back to the place they were stolen from. If you're caught handling stolen property, you're already halfway to jail, no matter who stole it.

I always knew from an early age not to commit the cardinal sin of leaving a trail of evidence behind me – I knew that anything from a footprint to a fancy silver necklace could and would be used to imprison me. After a long period undertaking daily robberies, I'd accumulated enough silver to be hung for. To minimise this danger, I regularly scheduled an afternoon of meltdown. Melting silver down to a lump of metal is simpler than it sounds and was accomplished by me, at home alone, but with the help of an "off-the-shelf" oxyacetylene kit. A straightforward operation, I'd lock all the doors in the house and in the kitchen and set up a metal bowl to drip the melt into. Then I'd heat a small handful at a time, waiting for it to turn, like butter. I'd melt enough handfuls to get a huge lump of molten metal so big it would take two of us to lift it out of the bowl. Only then did I relax. Only then could I be sure that no one would know where the silver came from. When it had cooled, we'd empty the big solid lump of silver from the bowl into a bed sheet to be wrapped up. Then, when we had the time and inclination, we'd pop it into a holdall bag and go by train to London to sell it (I went with either my brother Stephen because he had his own haul to get rid of, or with Bad Steve who liked to keep me company). We had a couple of places we sold to in Hatton Garden. I expect, as per usual, we were given what was probably a lot less than the market value. They would buzz us into their shop on street level and we'd put our haul onto the counter for them to inspect. "Sign in there, please," they'd say, and not even look at what name we put in the book. "Come back in a couple of hours." When we came back, they'd give us a price (£400, £800, £1,200). We'd accept whatever they said and get very drunk on the train home.

By consolidating my earnings from a series of robberies, I did very well. I'd served my time, in every respect. I had full freedom of movement in my hips, out on the roads (courtesy of Martin) and in business. I was fifteen years old with five grand in my pocket – so far as I was concerned, I'd come of age.

Having spent most of my active childhood wearing a girdle and hobbling about on crutches, it was hardly surprising I hankered after speed and travel – to go as far as I could, as fast as I could. To this end, I bought a car, a bright blue MGB. I can't describe the feeling of pride that ran through me when I held those keys for the first time. Sadly, still small in stature, I was too small to get behind the wheel. For fear of arrest and confiscation, I just drove up and down our street. Our Martin was honoured with the task of driving me around in it. Uncomfortable as it was for three boys to sit in, for longer than five minutes really, Bad Steve, Martin and me travelled all the way to Bristol Airport in it on the first leg of our journey to Tenerife for a much-deserved and much-needed holiday, all bought and paid for by me. My mother thought we'd won the holiday in a competition. Bad Steve's mum didn't question it – I think she was just glad that her son would get to experience a holiday she could never afford to take him on.

CHAPTER 6

Getting burned...

We flew Britannia Airways. There's a photo of me standing at the bottom of the steps of the plane. In it my hair is still long, my face still cute.

I'm wearing clothes bought from Cody, my favourite shop, exclusively designer label, stand-out smart and sold at prices that even I flinched at sometimes. I'm also wearing a watch bought with proceeds from robbing. Young, flying high without crutches or girdles now, not even my age could contain me. With an as yet unblemished career as a burglar, I felt I could at last enjoy some of the real fruits of my labour, untroubled by grown-ups and the rules and regulations they were so fond of. From crutches to bike to MGB to plane. I would never stand still again. Indeed, life was about to get a whole lot faster.

***

I wasn't prepared for the grill of the sun that hit us when we got off the aeroplane, nor the strength of the beer they sold us when we settled ourselves in at the hotel bar. It didn't take long for people to notice us. Because Bad Steve's bad language was so bad, we regularly got thrown out of bars, and we nearly got thrown out of the hotel the night we smashed in the balcony window in a drunken fit of fun-loving over-exuberance. We drank, we played, we enjoyed our freedom.

This holiday was, for me, more than just a fortnight on the piss. It represented a deeper, more personal journey – a dream realised, a milestone reached, a demonstration that my belief in my own power and sense of maturity had been neither misplaced nor exaggerated. And to celebrate, I got my hair cut. I now looked fifteen going on twelve. They still served me drinks at the bar, mind. Back home, they wouldn't have let me out of the children's area.

Besides getting drunk and dodging trouble, I used the freedom of foreign territory as fuel for my curiosity. I took time out alone to find out about the place, as a traveller, a boy let loose, a free spirit in his element.

Whilst I felt gratified that certain self-beliefs had been proven valid, I held other, equally strong and perfectly formed opinions about the world at large that were largely if not completely wrong, based as they were on the world according to a "still very small" boy from Swilly. So it didn't seem to me either strange or stupid to set off on a long walk in the midday sun in shorts and flip-flops with no hat on or map to guide me. I walked for miles. There was more to "foreign lands" than flash hotels and bilingual waiters who served food and drinks all day and all night if you so fancied. *Foreign* could be extremely unpredictable. On the roads that linked one holiday resort to another, it could also be eerily quiet. *Foreign* offered up dangers that were far beyond the terrain of my limited imagination. It struck me, rather late in the day, that for want of a glass of water, you could easily die in a foreign country and no-one would notice.

After my *"I'm just goin for a walk"* experience, I lay in bed for two days, sore from head to toe, and sun sick. For the first time in a long time, I had been forced to come to a halt. That time in bed allowed me to reflect on some of the bigger questions that crossed my mind from time to time. Sick as I was, I was immensely relieved to have discovered (for myself) a world beyond Swilly. I was proud of my achievements. I'd been told I wouldn't amount to much, that my future prospects were bleak. But I'd discovered that my future need not – and should not – be hemmed in by the expectations of people who had never taken a risk in their life. The merchant navy could have satisfied my taste for travel and adventure, but instead they had all chosen to focus on what I couldn't do. I had both the skill and the courage to create my own opportunities and to profit from them.

On the drive home from Bristol Airport to Plymouth, my new (used) MGB let us down. The fan belt bust. The police came by and took a look at us. They rang in to get the gen on us. They couldn't pull us. And they wouldn't help us. We had to sit like suckers on the motorway until eventually a lorry driver rescued us with a pair of tights he just happened to lay his hands on.

***

Once I got mobile proper, I got cocky. Martin and I continued to work as a team. Tony did his own thing, more of an opportunist than a schemer. Our Stephen would jet off to Jersey and Zurich every other week doing jewellery shops and doing well. He'd out-grown the South West by some distance. He was a face.

***

Our burgling enterprise was set up purely to fund the lifestyle we aspired to. To this end, I always looked to maximise profit. I learned to schedule and secure Martin's services in advance, to ensure a full day's graft, which in turn meant I had to be far more rigorous with my research and discovery. As always, we changed locations frequently to avoid recognition. We travelled far and wide across Devon and Cornwall and always took back routes, moorland roads, tiny lanes and cut-throughs to get from one place to another without being spotted and pulled over. Martin drove my MGB well, but not very fast. I knew that once *I* got behind the wheel proper, there'd be no stopping me. I understood the need for caution, but if and when it did come on top (they were onto us) I'd always prefer a chase to surrender.

We did all kinds of houses, cottages and mansions, three-bed semis and new builds. We did a large country pile belonging to a prominent local beak, relieving him of his family heirlooms for good. That was the job that put the regional crime squad onto high alert. They'd been onto our Stephen anyway – bored, he'd been involved in a number of shop robberies in Plymouth. The Old Bill had been round our house every day of the week on some pretext or other. On one visit, a very nosey copper spotted my bike leaning up against the wall in the dining room. I actually saw him spot it and watched the cogs of his little brain clicking over. I knew he'd be back, and he was. They arrested me for robbing a series of houses in Plymstock and for attempting to rob an old man of his jewels and household valuables. In their bid to nail me, they forced me to take part in ten ID parades.

Even with my new haircut, the old man managed to pick me out. He had me bang to rights, but none of the other victims were as smart. And so they interviewed me. They got nothing off me. No fear. No tears. No comment. And so they interviewed me some more.

"How can you sit there, cool as a cucumber? Look at you. You're not right, boy! You're not right in the head."

"No comment."

"You were seen. The old man's ID'd you… and your bike."

"No comment."

They had no other evidence. No jewels. No stolen goods. And, they complained, I was taking up an extraordinary amount of their time, young whippersnapper that I was. They wanted me as much as any of the most hardened and experienced criminals on their books. But, as luck would have it, my new haircut saved me and I was freed on a technicality.

Once again, I escaped justice. A close call, as I explained to our Tony, whose ears pricked up when I told him about the country house and the old man who lived there. He didn't miss a trick. He went back himself and robbed the place. Got a haul of antiques and silver candlesticks. It was, I suppose, a kind of revenge job, but it would have meant a lot more to me if our Tony had taken me with him. Still, I was chuffed. We were communicating man to man now, not big brother little brother. Tony had few words but a big heart, and I tried to emulate that spirit with our Martin because I really did appreciate his contribution.

***

Close calls never dampened my enthusiasm any. I carried on, business as usual, using our Martin as my driver. Because for the most part we were concentrating our efforts on jewellery, we didn't need to load or carry so much, and so we almost always went out in my MGB. It was a sad day when I had to say goodbye to that car, but there were a few other losses to mourn too, when the shit finally hit the fan. Losses that still have an impact on me now.

It was a bright and sunny day and so we drove to Cornwall, planning to spend the afternoon on the beach after our day's work was done and if all turned out well. We started off OK. We managed to rob an old woman's house of quite a haul. Our MO had become so well known I suspect the regional crime squad picked the job up as soon as the theft was called in. You can imagine the report: *Two lads, one still a minor, in and out the house in seconds, using a getaway sports car*. It shouldn't have been *that* hard to nail us, but still, they took their time. The weather turned on us, so there was no beach outing. We made our way back to Plymouth. Cornwall back then had more back lanes than main roads, so you could bump into coppers on patrol anywhere and everywhere. We got spotted and they gave chase. Instead of a chase, our Martin let them overtake us. They forced us to stop. I threw all the jewels underneath the passenger seat and ran off.

My brother took the rap. The coppers took my car and parked it up in Crownhill compound. They cut into the roof so the rain could get in and make the insides go all mouldy. They also took a cut of our takings. The list of "missing items" put forward in court and used to substantiate the seriousness of Martin's crime was incomplete, and by some margin – more than could be caused by simple error. Our Martin's solicitor gave me sight of all the paperwork, detailed descriptions of the items of jewellery we'd stolen. Only half the jewels that we'd actually taken were on it. In court, the police made a big deal out of the fact that the victim had been devastated by what had happened to her, the extent of the loss, the nature of it. Her life, we were told, would never be the same again. The jewels we'd stolen, and the precious memories they symbolised, could not be replaced. Our actions had destroyed any chance of this woman ever being able to feel safe again. In court, Martin was paraded as a savage with no moral code, a parasite preying on the weak and the vulnerable. Jury, I direct you to ask Her Majesty's screws to throw away the key.

Had I been solely to blame for this woman's misfortune I think I might have felt a lot worse than I did. But since the police themselves had dipped their sticky little fingers into the swag bag after it had been transferred over to them for safekeeping, I felt more anger than guilt, and no shame at all. It was dog eat dog. Even the police were at it.

This was my first experience of official unfair play. Up until this point, I'd respected the police as the good guys. They were the ones you could rely on to do things properly. I wanted some good guys out there, someone to reassure people like my mother that there were systems in place to keep her safe, someone to uphold the rule of law, to keep a proper score of what was really going on. Sadly, this is an illusion borne on a tide of what was probably a more respectable history. Of course, there were some good coppers about, and there still are, but they're not – and by some distance – all good.

Our Martin got four years and three months. The police all but demolished any belief I might have had in their system. It would cost them dear.

CHAPTER 7

My return to education….

Our Tony and me were the only ones left at home (not including Maureen, who just took herself off to school like a normal child) after Martin got captured. Our Stephen was either travelling doing jobs or being contained somewhere between jobs. I got on well with all my brothers, but I'd say Tony was the easiest, the gentlest of us. Whilst he wasn't an out and out thief like I was (he didn't hack it at Toshiba for long, mind), he was always up for any work that might bring him the money he needed to live it up with the ladies. So we hatched a plan. Without a car and a driver, and low on funds, we were forced to take to the streets once again.

A good burglar will always spend a lot more time on research than robbing. Finding empty houses is labour intensive. And as wise old Tony pointed out, full-grown men can't go round knocking on people's doors asking for directions and glasses of water. So we put our thinking caps on and decided we'd front up as *real* researchers. We bought clipboards and put jumpers on and pretended to be students from the local polytechnic. Our spiel went something like this… *"Do you have a cat, sir? Oh, two? Really? How often do you feed them? Our research is going to explore how much we love our pets and how much we spend on them. So, sir, how much does it cost to feed your cat every week?"*

Since neither Tony or me had stepped foot in a place of academic enquiry for quite some time (and we'd never even crossed the threshold of Plymouth Polytechnic, a huge block of new build slap bang in the city centre), it won't come as any surprise for you to learn that our "act" wasn't quite as convincing as it might have been. Tony looked far too cool to be clever and I was just too small. I should have been in my school uniform. Anyhow, someone smelt a rat, called the police and we got pounced on. Unbelievably, we were both refused bail – for carrying clipboards!?

Tony got sent to Dorset to a remand centre, and still not sixteen, I was shipped off to a children's home called Parklands in Plymouth, where I remained for only one evening. It was a splendid place with lovely gardens and no locks on the door. I could come and go as I pleased. In my naivety, and perhaps tired, having spent so long in a police cell, I never attempted to escape that night, preferring instead to chat to the children and later on to sleep. It was in Parklands where I first met Jim Millington, who you'll meet later.

STILL SMALL VOICE

***

EXTRACT FROM REPORT TO

PLYMOUTH JUVENILE COURT

24th April 1981

CONCERNING: David James Hill

D.O.B: 19.9.64

PREVIOUS: Burglary – no further action taken because of age.

Family:
Father   Deceased

Mother   Rosalie Mary Hill – housewife

Siblings: Stephen Hill
              Martin Hill
              Anthony Hill
              Maureen Hill

HOME:

Three-bedroomed council house in good condition and well furnished.

Mother:

Presents herself as concerned but somewhat overburdened mother, experiencing difficulty raising a large family by herself, etc.

Siblings   *Etc*

David

David was admitted to Neathern Brock Intermediate Treatment Centre in September 1980. Unfortunately, his response was largely negative and staff there indicate that they feel there is little hope of a long-term positive reaction from David.

David has a sense of self confidence about himself and handles himself well in stressful situations, e.g. police interviews and court appearances.

He can always supply an apparently rational reason for his involvement with the police, but there is always a feeling that he is only telling half-truths.

It is very unlikely that he can afford all his clothes and social habits, including holidays abroad, without some help from illegal funding, be it through his brothers or as a result of his own activities.

David can be plausible, likeable, friendly and responsive, but he reveals this side of his character only when necessary. It is difficult to be certain what the other side of David contains.

***

The following day, the powers that be, came to their senses and shipped me off to a place near Exeter called the Atkinson Unit, a secure lock-up for unruly teenagers who were not as interesting as they were dangerous. There were twelve beds for boys and girls aged ten to seventeen, and it was described by the social worker as a regional secure unit for observation and assessment.

***

The Atkinson Unit

Court Report

David Hill

DATE OF BIRTH: 19th September 1964

DATE OF ADMISSION: 3rd June 1981

David Hill was admitted to the Atkinson Unit on the 5th June 1981 and has been in residence for 152 days, pending today's court appearance.

The Atkinson unit is the regional secure unit for observation and assessment. It is a 12 bedded centre, opened in 1979, with accommodation for boys and girls aged 10 to 17. It has its own specialist support services, and a catchment area far beyond the environs of the south-west.

David is a young man aged 17 years one month, height 5'11", weight 10 stone and £10 and is in generally good physically health he is of slim, athletic build with dark hair and fresh complexion.

He is the youngest of five children and has been unemployed since leaving school at Easter of this year. He is clearly considerably influences by the attitudes and opinions of his three brothers.

David Hill has presented no behaviour problems whilst here. He has proved in the main cooperative and sensible, and has carried out instructions promptly and without question. He is an articulate and self-confident young man, generally average intelligence, and capable of in Crete impressing with the superficial charm and good manners.

However, very little of this young man's true nature has been revealed during this period of remand, and in my view beneath the plausible exterior lies a character who is devious, calculating and manipulative. I would consider him to have few scruples or principles and to be largely without conscience in his dealings with others.

Repeated attempts have been made to discuss with David Hill the nature of and reasons for his increasing delinquency that he has consistently refused to enter into any such dialogue.

If he is found guilty in court to the offences with which he is charged, I would suggest with respect that there is no alternative to a custodial sentence. Whilst it is unlikely that such a sentence would deter this young man from further transgressions, it would, however, serve to protect society for a period from his manipulative exploitations.

J.A. Gripit

Head of unit

30 October 1981

***

There were high walls and bars on the windows and more staff than kids. You couldn't get a minute's peace unless you were asleep. The seriously disturbed were shipped off to Manchester, as happened to

Micky D, a boy I met on my first day there. Micky couldn't settle (and perhaps never would), having stabbed his gran to death. It was no accident. Nor was it an angry outburst, a blinding moment of irrational aggression meted out in the midst of an exuberant temper tantrum. No. He stabbed her seventy-two times, which must have taken a fair amount of time, not to mention stamina. He only stayed with us for a few days. We were told his needs could be better met up north in a secure facility where the staff had been trained to use a ground-breaking colour card system as a mood-monitoring device. None of us were sad to see the back of him, it has to be said. In Manchester, every minute of his day would be captured and then categorised as a colour: red for anger, blue for calm, that kind of thing. Manchester was Madchester for us – if they sent you up there, you were pretty much past saving.

If the Devil makes work for idle hands, he didn't get much in the way of misbehaviour out of us lot. We were kept constantly entertained with a whole range of activities designed to inject in us a love of labour, learning and life in general. They chose our subjects on a case-by-case basis, ensuring we were put to work on projects that chimed with our particular bents and interests, and so I found myself spending a great deal of time in the woodworking unit, where I was taught how to construct my own crossbow. This wasn't a kid's crossbow. This was a proper man-sized crossbow complete with stock. With the application of what for me was painstaking patience, I stuck together hundreds of laminated strips of wood to create an object of finesse and beauty. I spent two months on this crossbow before the powers that be took it off me. I was, as you can imagine, not very impressed, to put it mildly, and to give him his due, neither was my woodwork tutor. He had been enjoying what for him was a rare success, engaging one of their "more difficult" and "vocal" students for what turned out to be an unprecedented amount of time. It ought to go without saying, but I'll say it anyway, after they took away my crossbow, all the trust he'd built up during this initial period of incarceration evaporated, along with my dream of becoming a world-class crossbow expert.

Things began to look up again when an old lady, a volunteer, befriended me. We shared an interest in jewellery, particularly silverware. She knew a great deal about it, the hallmarks, sources, relative quality, and so we hit it off, big time. I was on a roll again. She even brought pieces into the unit for me to see and analyse and learn from.

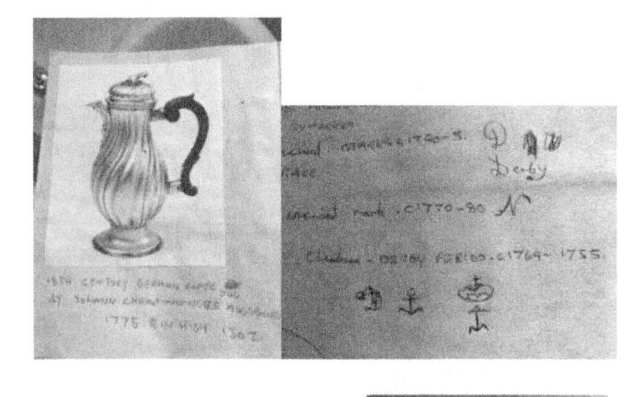

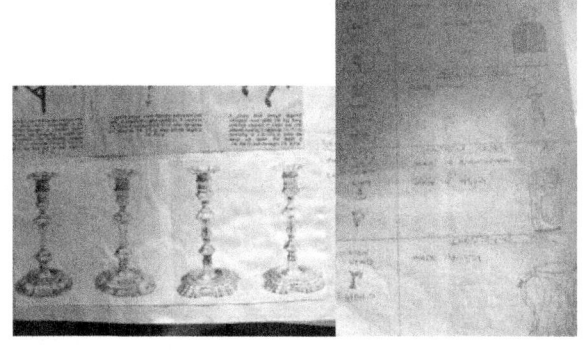

I was a bit rusty on the academic front, but she was very patient with me and me with her. As soon as I found my feet, I became a very fast learner. She brought in scrapbooks to teach me all about the different symbols I'd be likely to come across in the jewellery trade and their relative worth on the market, depending on the item's age and place of manufacture. I learned from her that an anchor mark was from Birmingham, whilst the head of a lioness denoted a London maker. As education goes, this really *was* highly personalised and relevant to my workplace.

You'd think it couldn't get much better than this but it did. Before long we had another tutor teaching us how to make our own wine.

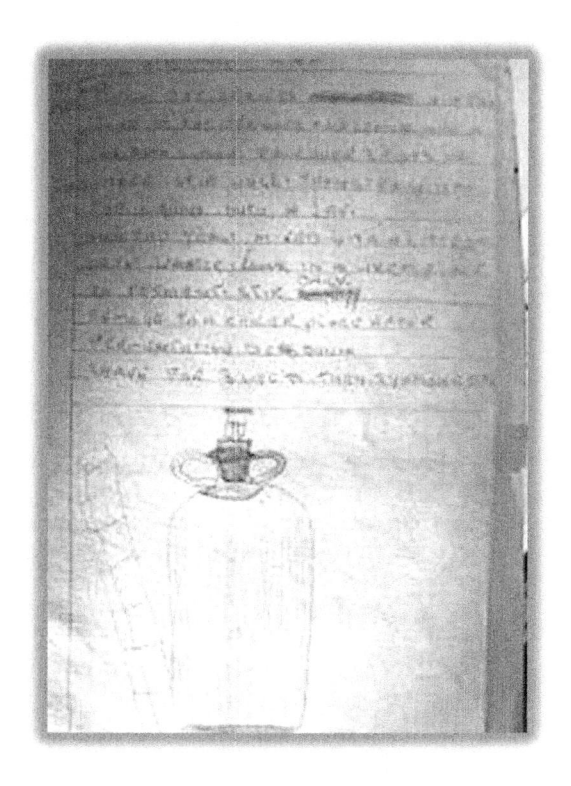

We learned all about the chemical reactions that created the alcohol and how this could be adapted depending on the fruit or the vegetable and the fermentation processes peculiar to each. We each had our own sample wine-making kits for demonstration purposes. Like the crossbow saga, we were given a very long time to engage with and enjoy this learning – six weeks in fact – before the taps were shut off and our brew was taken away. Once again, I kicked off.

Aside from these major cock-ups, we weren't treated too badly in the Atkinson Unit, but that's not to say I didn't think about getting out of there every minute of the day I was in there. I had to be patient and wait until my court case before I'd even get any indication of what my final sentence was likely to be. I spent many months doing just that, and all the while, my prized MGB was sitting in the compound at Crownhill in Plymouth going mouldy.

Our Stephen took some time out and put his busy international career as a jewel thief on hold to come and pay me a visit. He brought me a birthday present – a Sony Walkman and Pink Floyd's *The Wall* on tape.

Solitary

When the day came, the judge threw the book at us! We were done for conspiracy to rob, fraudulently presenting as college students, and in addition, we got done for robbing a judge's house months earlier – a job they'd been trying to pin on us for some time. My bike had given the game away. The judge who dealt with us said, "If I could give you five years, I would. But I can't." He gave me nine months in borstal instead, all of which I had to serve, every last minute of it. My time in the Atkinson Unit was not classed as "remand" and so it didn't get subtracted from my sentence. Worse still, none of the good behaviour I'd been keen to impress them with whilst I was in there had been noted, counted or admired by anyone except me.

Our Tony also got borstal, but they sent him to a place called Guys Marsh, fifty miles away from Portland where I was locked up. In Portland, much of my time was spent in my cell, and the rest of it marching across the parade grounds. There was a serious lack of freedom here, and in part, I was glad of my solitary confinement, not least because the young men who were in this place had been sent there because of their "violent" nature. Why they'd sent me there, I don't know. I couldn't have been less violent, standing around on street corners with a jumper on, clutching a clipboard.

Alone in my cell, I did become anxious as each long day impressed on me the extent and intensity of the gloom I'd been sentenced to, nine months of it. No fun at all. Never had I confronted such bleakness. When I heard a friendly tap-tap on the pipe from the cell next door, I felt a visceral relief, as if someone had unblocked me.

"I'm John. What's your name? D'yer smoke? D'yer wanna fag?"

He passed little roll-ups through to me and I learned how to scar my lungs with nicotine, which was far more interesting than lying on my bed looking at the ceiling.

Morning. Marching. Lock-up. Sleep. Fag. Lunch. Marching. Sleep. Lock-up. Association. Fag. Sleep. Morning.

I have never been very fond of marching, or military culture in general. The prison officers in charge of the marching were drunk on their power, as any fool would be, forcing grown men with hungry minds to parade in front of them as a set of *mindless* clockwork toy soldiers. Our Tony was having a much better time of it in Guys Marsh, I learned (and I didn't learn much else, except how to smoke). It was by far the softer option – "a holiday camp" in fact. Well, the shouting and spitting couldn't have been any worse. And the undercurrent of tension no more oppressive either. Portland Borstal was a proper prison but with kids in it – they made no concessions. Get your head down. That was all you could do.

I made some enquiries. I asked why a peaceful boy like me was being forced to mix with such a dangerous and violent group of criminals? How was this going to help me?

Good job I asked. That same week, I was sent to meet with the governor.

"Hill. You're not supposed to be here."

"Am I not, sir?"

"You've been sent here by error."

"Is that so, sir?"

"Stop asking me questions."

"Sir?"

"What?"

"What error, sir?"

"It says here that you were responsible for a serious violent attack and absconded on being apprehended. I looked in your notes to get more details so I could ascertain how dangerous a prisoner you might be, and lo and behold, I find no evidence to support the allegation. Someone has made a mistake."

"So can I go 'ome then, sir?"

"Home? You've been sentenced to nine months. You've only been here a fortnight."

Worth a try.

"No, you're to pack up your things and get ready for transfer. We're sending you to Guys Marsh."

Not before they'd marched me around the parade ground a few more times and let me stew in my cell for three more days did they make any attempt to act on the governor's instructions and transfer me.

CHAPTER 8

It's the cream that rises to the top...

Just as the second hand on a clock carves up time into tiny, tiny pieces, so jail slices up your life into a million mindless moments. There aren't any wide-open spaces or long periods of time to get comfy in. There is very little opportunity to experience any long-sweeping smooth flows of movement. Any hint of flow is disrupted by noise or bodies or doors swinging into your face. There is exercise time, play time, sleep time, work time, learning time, eating time. Lying-in-bed-wondering-what's-going-on back-home time. I didn't spend too long on that. Truth is, you can't do anything for very long in prison. The only thing that endures is time itself.

So any break in the monotony was welcomed. And a transfer to somewhere else was like Christmas come early. We travelled from Portland nick to Guys Marsh by car. I enjoyed that journey a lot. I relished every second of my release from the confines of a cell. The driver was enjoying himself too, taking bends as I would have, fast, no breaking, driving into them with confidence and dash. I had my window open full so I could drink in the thrill of freedom from the countryside, so green, undulating, far-reaching. It felt a bit like being in someone else's film.

When the car finally stopped, that illusion of freedom was replaced with the thud of brutal reality. We drove into a compound, bare but for an ugly regiment of World War II Nissen huts with metal corrugated roofs. There was no sign of life anywhere. They might have been tombs. This was Guys Marsh Borstal, my home for eight months and two weeks.

The impact of this contrast in fortunes struck me hard, having just spent more than an hour contemplating the merits of the countryside. Now I was being led calmly and quietly to the reception hut, a screw in front and one behind me. They didn't bait me or befriend me. They did their job and I did mine. I was to submit to their order, their rules, their way of doing things.

I sat in reception (the reception hut was some distance from the rest of the prison) waiting for my induction. At the other end of the hut a door opened and a convict appeared out of nowhere, a thin wiry man with curly blond hair and big red lips, Mick Jagger style. He also had a large patch of acne worrying his chin. I knew him. He was from Plymouth, a mate of our Martin. John. Older than me. Nearer twenty.

He had a mug of tea in one hand and a piece of cake in the other. He was just strolling around the place, like he was at home. He sighted me from way off and walked over to speak to me.

"Seen your Tone yet?"

"No," I said. "I jus' got 'ere."

"He's a diamond he is."

"Is he OK?"

"He's gettin' on with it. It ain't 'ard. It's like fuckin' boardin' school, mate."

"'Oliday camp I was told?"

"Well there's no beer, no birds and no bus home, mate, so I think you're gonna be disappointed."

Another man appeared in the same doorway John came through. This one wore a blue jumpsuit with "TRUSTEE" written in red across his chest. He sidled up behind John and tapped him on the shoulder.

"Time you was back in your class, mate."

John ignored him but pointed his thumb backwards. "He thinks he's a fuckin' screw."

"I'm the induction leader, *actually*."

"He's gonna in*duct* yer."

"I hope it don't 'urt!" I laughed at the pair of them.

"You need to pick up your kit first. Come wi' me. John, do as you're told an' get back to yer classroom or they'll come lookin' for yer."

The trustee with his "induction instruction file" under one arm tried to move John out of the way with his other. John put on a performance for me. He turned and smashed his mug of tea into the trustee's face. This attack drew blood. The trustee ran off.

"Ask him to put you down for Dorset House, then they might put you in Tone's dorm. You don't wanna be in with the Wessex lot coz they're all dickheads and nonces."

John just wanted to give me a more truthful induction, one that meant something, and I appreciated it. He carried on chatting as if nothing had happened, but I could see screws milling around and then they spotted him...

"John, John, they're on to you. Behind you..."

But he wasn't interested. He liked the sound of his own voice too much. He was mid flow when a screw grabbed him by the arm and took him away. The trustee returned, pressing toilet paper to his chin, like he'd cut himself shaving. He led me through to the canteen.

In there, two screws were sitting down drinking tea and smoking, using a saucer for an ashtray, which I've never liked. They weren't in uniform. They looked like office workers in shirts and ties. When they saw me, one jumped up.

"Here he is now. Hill, innit? Wanna cup of tea, lad?"

"Yes please."

"Piece o' cake?"

"Don't mind if I do," I said. "Can I choose?" I went over to the counter.

Behind it, way out of my reach, there was a table serving as a shop, and on it, the stock was arranged neatly, in sections, like a child's idea of a shop. There was a selection of sweets and biscuits, teabags, jars of coffee and piles of tobacco stacked high. These could all be bought with the wages that were paid to the inmates at the end of the week, amounting to no more than a quid, one fifty at best, I was told. All this stuff could be bought... or it could be nicked, was my thinking.

Still dithering over Jaffa Cakes or Battenberg, I surveyed the security. We were at the far end of the hut, separated from the rest of it by a wall of plasterboard. The door into the canteen was Chubb locked. On my side, there were big padlocks on the counter shutters, and on theirs, big Chubb locks on the doors. On our side, the windows were too small. Outside the hut, there was a lot of traffic, screws and inmates, back and forth to classrooms and the offices, etc. Too risky to even contemplate, not even at night – no, especially at night. On their side of the counter, there was just one small window that didn't face onto the main grounds, but it was so small you'd be stuck trying to get the head of a small child through it.

I sat down at a different table to the screws and waited for my tea and cake to be served. Different kettle of fish all this was, compared to Portland. Cake be damned. Whilst I ate my Battenberg, I watched the trustee take his papers from his file so he could read the rules at me. He was squinting at the pages.

"You blind or summat?"

"Lost me glasses. Well, they got smashed. New ones ain't turned up yet."

"Someone else smack you, did they?"

"You need to sign here." He pushed some pages at me. Treating me like I was a kid.

"You just grassed my mate John up, did you?"

"No, I never. The screw asked me how come I was bleeding."

"An' they just go straight for him then?"

"They know what he's like."

"What's your name then?"

"Binsy."

I signed his bits of paper but I never read any of them. "I'll be lookin' out for you, Binsy."

"I'm not a grass."

"You seen our Tone in here? Tony Hill?"

"You 'is brother?" He looked scared. Our Tony wasn't a violent man, but that didn't matter. Our Stephen's reputation alone – he'd spent half his youth in this place – was enough cover for the lot of us.

"I've got to 'and this file over to the screw now. It's what happens. I'm not a snitch."

He was asking for permission. "Well go on then."

I watched him hand the induction file over. The screws were still smoking and drinking tea. The screw who'd signed for my tea and cake came over and sat down next to me. He rattled off a load of information and, except for what he had to say about meal times and suicide, none of it sunk in. I was wondering how long it would take for me to lift those fags out of the canteen.

***

Gone fishing

Tony and me got to work on the job right away. First task was to find some decent tools to use to get in there. Gripper the groundsman helped us out. It was a pleasure to get one over on him.

Gripper was Welsh, middle-aged and old school. Lads were to be put to work and disciplined, and after a few years of this sort of treatment they'd come to realise that crime doesn't pay. He wasn't on duty with us every day, but when he was, this was how he introduced himself. And at volume.

"HILL 038 – GET A CLOTH AND SOME GLITTO AND DO THE INSIDE AND OUTSIDE OF THE PANS, AND WHEN YOU'RE DONE, COME AND SHOW ME."

I was the one he picked on. I don't know why he had it in for me. And I didn't spend a great deal of time trying to work out why, either – I never gave screws much thought at all. Like bad weather, you just had to put up with them. I used to take the piss out of Gripper – doing impressions of his Welsh accent for the lads.

"HILL 038. GET SOME CLOTH AND SOME GLITTO AND DO THE INSIDE AND OUTSIDE OF THE PANS."

The pans were toilet pans. He expected me to clean each and every one, by hand, inside and out. No one else got this job when he was on – just me. And every time.

"HILL 038 – GET A CLOTH AND SOME GLITTO AND DO THE INSIDE AND OUTSIDE OF THE PANS, AND WHEN YOU'RE DONE, COME AND SHOW ME."

Some of those bogs were shit-high, and I for one wasn't going at them with my bare hands.

At the end of each dorm there were cupboards for storing cleaning equipment, like mops and brushes, and occasionally you'd find a toilet brush in there. There was no guarantee, mind. All four main dorms shared the cleaning equipment, and so the brush could be on any one at any time. There was a reluctance to store any number of tools or equipment that could be used as a weapon. Only trustees and staff had keys to the cleaning cupboards, and so it was upon me to find one of these trustees and get them to search for a toilet brush whenever the toilets were too shitty for me to deal with.

"Binsy, giz the key to the cupboards an' I'll bring 'em right back."

"Can't do that. You know I can't."

"Binsy..."

He had his glasses back on now. We'd become mates, kind of. I looked after him and protected him from the likes of John from Plymouth who used little people as a punchbag. I've never enjoyed mindless violence. It reeks of cowardice to me.

"What are you doin' 'ere?" said Gripper, catching us idling in the hall of our Nissen hut. "HILL 038," he shouted, "GET THE CLOTH AND THE GLITTO..."

"I am, sir."

Gripper got called away. Binsy went through his keys looking for the one I needed.

"What else you got keys for there?"

"Not tellin' yer."

"Binsy!"

He had keys to all kinds of cupboards I learned, not just for cleaning materials. I got him to give me a tour one day. The gardening shed held promise, and so I got him to start right there. I was right. In there, I found an old fishing net amongst a tray of twine and sandpaper and suchlike. It had holes in and was useless. Could be used to catch a half ounce of Old Holborn though, I was sure. Not a problem. We also found some bamboo sticks in the corner. They were being used for planting peas and suchlike. I took the net and a bamboo stick back to our dorm, and me and Tony united them with twine to create a long and strong lifting net. Our next problem was timing.

Lunchtimes, everyone was forced out of dorms to the refectory. Trustees remained in the dorms to ensure all the lads had gone. That was their job. We nabbed Binsy and told him he was wanted elsewhere.

He knew it was better to comply than resist, not because we'd beat the crap out of him – on the contrary, he considered me fair. I didn't terrorise or bully him. I used him. When I didn't need him, I left him well alone. Whilst I could and did keep the dogs off him, he knew I could just as easily not bother. Fear can be better than a thump if you want to beat up on someone. I could do *fear* really well.

So Binsy made sure all the lads had gone for dinner and then came over to the canteen with us to stand guard. Screws and inmates all ate at the same time – only trustees were out and about and so wouldn't attract suspicion if seen. We smashed the small window behind the canteen and put our net through. It was easily long enough. It was a bit like being at the fair. We got a decent haul quite quickly.

As a trustee, Binsy had his own cupboard, again under lock and key. His job was to take into safekeeping any valuables, like watches or rings, etc. whilst the lads were swimming or playing football. We put the haul of fags inside Bins' cupboard, taping them to the roof so they couldn't be seen on a casual inspection. Job done.

When the crime was discovered, there was a lot of whispering and finger-pointing. Even the screws were under suspicion. I did very little to stop the rest of the lads from believing *I* was responsible. I wanted the recognition. And it wasn't long before I got it. They arrested me and Tony and took us down the block. One after the other, a screw took us aside in a bid to seduce us into turning supergrass. I had to laugh. Tony wasn't so amused. He'd done a lot more bird than me by this time. He'd seen it all. He was *tired,* all over. He had *tired* washed into his jumper.

They searched our cell. The rule was, if they found you with stolen goods they'd send you straight to Portland. Whilst leniency of the kind we were subject to in Guys Marsh can work like a softened club being consistently bashed against your head, causing extreme annoyance and irritability, I didn't much fancy the bleakness and brutality of Portland again. I certainly didn't fancy all that marching around and being shouted at all the time.

The screws got gnarly and turned the whole place over. They unlocked Binsy's cupboard and gave it the once over but didn't go over it close enough. We got away with it. Or so I thought.

The following week they sent me to the dentist, who drilled seven fillings into my teeth. Seven fillings I didn't need.

There was no wall keeping us in. The fence was two foot high. If you absconded, you could pretty much guarantee that when they caught you – and you knew they would – they'd double the bird and treble the misery. So I got on with my sentence with the full intent of getting out and enjoying my freedom at the earliest possible opportunity. My goal was and always had been freedom. Whilst I did have my moments, I couldn't see much value in becoming a target for screws or inmates or anyone else who didn't have my best interests at heart.

I did welding and got a certificate – I was a dab hand at using oxyacetylene torches anyhow, without their help. I did a motor mechanics course, which I figured would come in handy, and my diligence was rewarded with a City and Guilds. And I got a painters and decorators certificate, which hasn't proved to be of much use to be honest, but we had a great laugh doing it, in slapstick Laurel and Hardy fashion. We even managed to bounce a pot of white paint off our painting platform so it flew and landed right on the napper of a passing screw. Not only did he get covered head to foot, he then slipped on the slick and put his back out. He was on the sick for weeks. We couldn't have planned it any better.

***

In the driving seat...

Summer 1981. I came out of borstal the same day as Tony. We went straight to the Camel's Head pub as soon as we got to Plymouth. Bad Steve was in there with his brother, Chris. Fran the barmaid didn't want to serve me.

"He ain't old enough. No way is he old enough."

We just ignored her. I had graduated, grown up. I was one of the men now. Seeing so many old friends and faces and feeling so at home, this move into adulthood was quiet, easy and welcome. I was my own man. No one bothered to ask me what my plans were. I was a burglar. That was my job. Cheers to that!

I could hardly foster much in the way of ambition conducting my burgling career on a bicycle – the only legal form of transport I could make use of. I passed my driving test on my second attempt in 1983 – important for me in some respects, a badge of competence certainly, but not for driving. I'd already driven thousands of miles without the badge or lessons or insurance, and most of the time without the owner's consent, so being granted permission to drive was hardly going to change my life very much. Having a driving licence did prove I wasn't thick or slow, and importantly allowed me to buy, sell and hire cars more easily.

My first company car, registered in my name, was a Mark 1 Ford Escort 1300GT – a mate sold it to me. Later on in my career I'd change cars fast and frequently to avoid detection, but I kept hold of this one for a while. It was quick, nippy, and held the road. One day, after I'd burgled a house alone, I was on my way home in it, sitting in traffic in Plymouth. I always locked the doors of the car when I was driving. And when I'm sitting in traffic, I always leave enough space behind the car in front to allow me to pull out and shoot off, if needs be. This particular day, I had stopped at some traffic lights when a police car came up behind me. I could see him looking rather too carefully at my plates. Then, he jumped out of his car, ran over to me and grabbed at my door handle. I engaged the clutch and gas and drove off, squealing at high speed. I went through a few red lights and round a few bends before abandoning the car in the middle of the road so I could run away, taking my parcel of silver with me. I ran through Ham Woods and chucked the jewellery into some bushes so I could go home. The next day, I reported my car stolen and went down to the police pound to collect it. I drove back to the woods to get my jewellery but it had gone. I was gutted. A day's work wasted. But at least I got my car back. I paint the picture because I went through this kind of routine fairly often – recce, rob, run...

If I wasn't out burgling, then I'd be in the Camel's Head pub, plotting. The building's gone now, levelled. Back then, it was our community centre. Some of the most important events in my life took place in there. It wasn't the kind of pub you'd end up in by accident. The decor, the clientele, the building – any ordinary man would steer clear.

Even though I only became a Camel's Head regular after my stint in Guys Marsh, I was already a face by virtue of my family connections. But for some, it has to be said that I was still a *strange* face.

One day, I was sitting in there waiting on someone. I was daydreaming, pulling horsehair stuffing out of one of the seats next to me. There was a group of lads in there, strange to me. They were making quite a noise on the other side of the room, and every now and again their bad language would seize my attention. I'd look up and then look away and go back to my daydreaming. One of the lads walked over and stood next to me, too close, right over me. He bent down and took some of this horsehair stuffing from the chair for himself. He looked at it and then looked back at his mates, who were all standing stock still, silent. Then he grabbed my head and stuffed a great big handful of this stuff straight into my mouth.

I'm quite a cheerful soul really – I don't like nasty. Whether in or out of prison, I never used violence or the threat of violence to get my way, and as a result, I rarely fell victim to it. I was only ever violent when provoked. I was Mr Charisma on a good day, and very clear about my disapproval on a bad one. I was hardly a saint, and my reluctance to fight wasn't by any means a moral position. I just knew that by keeping a low profile I'd be able to get on with my burgling career undisturbed and without distraction. That said, I was happy to give someone a good hiding when they deserved it. And when someone really got to me, I got back to *them* fairly quickly. My stature had grown somewhat, having spent months on three meals a day. I was a late shooter. Having been embarrassingly small for my age, without a girdle to restrict me, my bones seemed to have revelled in their freedom and put me on an accelerated growth programme that surpassed my wildest dreams and expectations. I was already a big bloke when this medium-sized bloke decided to fill my mouth with seat stuffing.

I was stunned for a few seconds, to be honest. Still coming to terms with what had happened, I watched this lad have the gall to turn his back on me so he could have a good laugh with his mates, who were all jeering and clapping on the other side of the pub. So I took the opportunity to smash him in the head with my fist, and with so much force, he fell to the ground hard, instantly. On his journey down, he managed to detach a rack of pool cues from the wall. One of the cues almost landed in my hand, so I used this to batter him. The rest of the cues had landed in a mesh across the floor and my victim lay there amongst them, squirming whilst I tried to hit him a good one over the head, fast, bang... bang... bang, with the cue. His laughing mates had stopped laughing now. They shuffled off out the door whilst I used all the force and violence I could muster to make my point. But I kept missing him. The cue split and shattered, so all I was left with was a jagged shard to stab him. And I still missed! Now I look back, I can see how fortunate he was, but also how lucky I was too – had I found my target, it's unlikely he'd have lived. I finished him off with a good kicking. His body lay motionless against a backdrop of pool cues. His face was bruised and bloody. He looked like a painting.

Meanwhile, Jo Tooley, an old hand who sat in the same corner of the pub day in, day out (he'd been drinking in the Camel's Head since the day it first opened and many joked had not been home since), got up out of his chair and staggered over to have a word with me. He pointed his finger at me. He wasn't a happy man.

"What's all this? What's all this?" He was hissing through his teeth like a riled cat. "You're out of order! Do you 'ear me, lad? You're out o' bloody order! Look at the state o' this pool cue... you've buggered it. You know how much they cost, lad? Y'any idea?"

He bent down to pick up the rest of the cues that were scattered across the floor, stepping carefully around the injured man in case touching the body might contaminate him in some way.

***

The Camel's Head served us well as a community centre, for buying and selling, hiring and firing, plotting jobs, hatching schemes and sourcing opportunities. The pub landlord and his wife Fran were broad-minded enough to ignore much of what went on in there. But they could be selective – moody. I sold a car in there one day but got myself lumbered with a cheque – it was *cheque or no deal* so I *had* to go with it, but I didn't have a bank account. So I asked Fran if she'd do me the honours. She took my cheque but explained I'd have to wait a while *and* pay for the service. I didn't mind. I wasn't going anywhere and neither was she.

The day I went in to collect, there was utter bedlam in the pub. There was no one behind the bar or in front of it. There was a gang of underage kids fighting in one corner, a girl on the floor crying her eyes out in another, and everyone else was drunk, stoned, off their nuts and past caring. It wasn't even midday. I wanted my money and a drink, and so I waited and waited, and after a good long while I decided to help myself. I jumped up and over the bar, found myself a glass, and went to pour myself a drink. And then Bob appeared, Fran's husband.

"What you doin'?"

"What's it look like I'm doin'? I've been waitin' for ages."

"My wife's cashin' you a cheque an' you jus' come waltzin' in 'ere an' start nickin' the beer. How grateful are you then?"

"I'm not nickin' the beer."

"No, it doesn't look like it. Fuck off back behind the bar where you belong or I'll bar you, d'you 'ere me?"

"Bar me?"

"You 'eard."

"You serious?"

"You're barred, all right! That serious enough for yer?"

That night, me and Bad Steve waited until Bob'd locked up and then broke in. I wasn't after his takings. I just wanted to scare him. He always parked his car in a drive that you could only get at from the back of the pub, and from the inside. We broke in, got into his drive and poured a gallon of petrol all over his Ford Capri. Then we blew it up. Bad Steve lost his eyebrows on that one.

The next day I lost no time going back in there to ask Bob to pull me a pint.

"You're not really barred, David. I was only kidding."

***

Stephen, Martin, Tony and me. The four brothers. The Hill family. Solid, sure of ourselves, savvy. Martin liked his clothes and his cars and fed his habit, taking any and every opportunity he could to do so. Stephen was more of an entrepreneur. He did big jobs to satisfy his big ambitions. In the jewellers, he was able to lift a diamond right under the nose of a sales assistant, making himself almost invisible. Out on the street his bad attitude and sense of humour failure meant you could spot him from a mile away – he was a trouble magnet. Our Tony was always more interested in women and wearing the best clobber than developing a talent for robbery, and whilst he could hold his own in a brawl, he had no passion for fighting. I was the only one who had a strong and unwavering determination to earn as much as I could for as little effort as possible and on a daily basis. But our Stephen could and did top me in terms of the size of his hauls – it wasn't unusual for him to lift £50,000 worth of jewels on one job. I was the most successful in the long run. Not that any of us considered it a race even, or competition. We weren't a team either though. We each had our own act. From time to time we would join forces if and when an opportunity presented itself, and then it felt great to have brothers to play with, men I could trust, people who instinctively cared about me. And in this respect our Tony came top – he was easy, gentle and, when it came down to it, as opportunistic as the rest of us.

My brother Stephen's reputation was such that I felt protected from the most volatile characters who lived and operated around our neighbourhood, and I'm sure that without him and the backup of my other brothers I'd have received far more unwanted attention from these undesirables than I did. Stephen taught me a lot. He gave me a good foundation of knowledge, which I used to build on, and with all the passion, eagerness and attention to detail of a grade A student. Aside from a basic education in stones and gold, clocks and hallmarks, he taught me the value of discretion, concentration and focus. I looked up to him as a kid, but once I turned adult (I consider my graduation from borstal as the key marker of that transition), I no longer needed or looked for guidance from his quarter. I was my own man. That's not to say I didn't value or love my brothers. They were not unimportant. We were very close and loyal to one another. But we were, in many ways, a family of islands.

Our Stephen gave me the knowledge I needed to rob the right stuff and sell it. Our Martin helped me to serve my apprenticeship by driving me wherever I needed to go. Our Tony was more of a mate, and the camaraderie between us was strong. He showed me how to be stylish, cool, and he gave me the courage I needed to talk to the woman who would later become my wife. My wife. And where did I meet her? You guessed it, in the Camel's Head.

CHAPTER 9

On my return home from borstal, Mum accepted me as a full-grown thief along with all her other sons. She didn't make a fuss. She certainly didn't bother wasting any of her time trying to lecture me. The damage was done and she knew it.

I got to work right away. I did a few burglaries with Bad Steve, Tony and Martin, but I worked alone more often than not. I liked working on my own. I loved to drive. The love of speed, planted early on in a boy who was forced to walk through his childhood on crutches, has never left me. The car was an extension of my personality and the roads the crazy runways of a mind that needed constant stimulation, change, challenge and fun. Aside from periods of captivity, I have never been without a car, and in those days I tested every vehicle I drove to destruction. I drove Minis, Escorts, Capris and Cavaliers, Fiats and Fiestas – a different car every week was the norm – making it harder for the police to keep tabs on me. For additional safety, whenever I finished a job, I always drove home the quiet way, through lanes and across moors, up back alleys and down private driveways. I can drive in my sleep better than most people manage with their eyes wide open. I love it.

My wife-to-be was impressed when she found out that I owned my own car. She said yes straight away when I asked her out. Nineteen years old, she was standing at the bar with a mate in the newly named *Submarine*. It will always be the *Camel's Head* pub to me. She was the full package – blond and beautiful. She looked well brought up and comfortable in her own skin, not overly self-conscious, like so many girls her age seemed to me to be.

I said to our Tony, "She's nice." Just me saying this was a big step. I was admitting out loud that I had a yearning, a desire to be close to someone lovely, someone warm and gentle. I'd never done that before. Said it out loud.

"Git on then, our David. Get after her."

Whilst I had to work hard to conquer all my fears and embarrassment, our Tony found the whole flirting business effortless. He loved girls as much as I loved cars. He could get *any* woman he wanted. He had many. Never the same one twice though. Unlike me, he was neither nervous nor afraid of rejection. I'd had a few girlfriends before, but not many and not for long. My very first girlfriend let slip she wanted to marry me. I used to feed her Knickerbocker Glories on our days out together – she figured me for a mug. She started on about weddings and wouldn't let up – I was only thirteen years old. I didn't risk a romance again for several years. I just didn't have much interest in girls. Only Lydia. She is and always has been the one.

Lydia

I got pneumonia when I was a baby and they thought I'd die, so my dad, being Catholic, scheduled the baptism and last rites on the same day. I was only a few weeks old. Later on, I was christened Church of England because my mum was C of E. I expect they had a row about it – my mum and dad had horrible fights. I remember seeing her smash up his piano with a hammer. That said, she was lovely to us – the kids. She idolised us. When she got mad, she went for it, but most of the time she was laid-back and easy-going, and I think I probably take after her.

Both my grandmothers died early from TB. My mum was one of eight, and her mum and dad had lived in Plymouth all their lives. My maternal grandma was fifty-four when she went, long before I was born. After she died, some of her children went to Barnardo's and some to the war, but my mum never went anywhere – Grandad kept hold of her.

My paternal grandparents were Irish and moved to England just before my dad was born, their third son. After *his* mum died, his dad married again and his new wife, Lena, got pregnant very quickly. She wouldn't take Grandad *and* the three boys, so my dad and his two brothers were sent to an orphanage run by nuns in Liverpool. Such was the treatment they got there, they spent all their time escaping, but they were always found and taken back again. My dad told us some horrible stories about nasty nuns in Liverpool. My dad managed to escape for good when he was fourteen. He lived on the streets with his eldest brother, Martin. They were very protective of each other. To make ends meet, Martin joined the army and my dad the merchant navy. That's why he ended up in Plymouth.

I remember living in a council house just outside St Budeaux, but we gave this house up to move into my grandad's three-bedroom house – a ruse I think to get something a bit better. About a year later, we were given a four-bedroom house and then Grandad came to live with us, sleeping in the dining room. We all had our own bedrooms.

My dad became a hard-working faithful family man and, living so far away, lost touch with his brothers and his father. When I was sixteen, there was a knock at the door and my Uncle Martin was standing there. Mum and dad had gone to Torremolinos on holiday. After making such an effort, this was a bit of a let-down for him, but he didn't give up – he came back a few days later. They organised a family reunion with Pete the middle brother and Grandad. Lena was still married to him. Just after that, Grandad died. My maternal grandad was the only grandparent still living by the time I reached eighteen.

I've got three sisters, Rosie, Cathy, Valerie, and a brother. I'm the youngest. Mum went through fourteen pregnancies to get five children who lived. That must have been hard, but she came through it all with an easy attitude. She'd give you her world, my mum. Anything, so long as we were happy. If I wanted to go to the fair or the cinema, she'd empty out her purse for me. She was always there for us. We were fed well and dressed well, always in clean clothes, and me being the baby, I never wanted for anything.

My dad was strict. Raised by nuns, he was bound to be. He wanted us to know right from wrong, good from bad, to be respectful, to stay on the right path. He was religious. Not so devout it defined him, but he believed in God and he went to church. He was protective of his family, and like Mum he always stood by us. We all got on – all the kids. We still live around the corner from each other today.

I grew up to be a sheltered, naive and happy teenager.

David

Lydia reckoned that I only went up to her for a bet. But that's not true. As I say, I fancied her right off. I spotted her through the fog of that smoke-filled room. I was further encouraged by her friend Marian, who let it be known (whilst Lydia wasn't there) that my attentions would not go unrewarded. This was the green light I needed, and so when she came back and sat down on her bar stool, I went and asked her for a dance, a slow one. After it, we agreed to meet up the next day, the following morning in fact. It was a Sunday.

I'd forgotten I'd already arranged to go out the next day with Chrissie (Bad Steve's brother), Bill Roberts, and his dogs, a lurcher and Jack

Russell. We were going to Dartmoor, rabbiting. I didn't change my plans. Bill had also copped off the night before – with Lydia's mate Marian. So we went to pick *her* up first but couldn't find the house. So we were very late by the time we got to Lydia's. She was all dolled up, her face clogged with make-up. She wore stilettos, a short red mini-skirt and a white top.

"Sorry I'm late. Jump in." I held the door open for her, being gallant.

"Where we goin'?"

"Rabbitin'"

"Where to?"

"Out on the moor."

Between seeing her off the dance floor the night before and then arriving at her house on that Sunday morning, she'd somehow managed to chop all her hair off. It looked horrible. She reminded me of a budgie.

"Ow'm I s'posed to go rabbitin' in these?" She lifted up a leg to show me.

"Well, they might come in 'andy if we want to stab 'em to death maybe?"

Not the kind of first date she'd imagined, but she never complained. Lydia is not a complainer, which is one of her best qualities. I'm not saying she's a walkover or a victim because she really isn't. She just doesn't waste her breath on things she knows she can't change. Bill's Jack Russell jumped straight into her lap as soon as she got in.

We parked up at the cafe on the edge of Dartmoor, just past Roborough, and set off on foot across rough terrain in search of our quarry. We walked for miles, for ages. I think it must have been quite tricky in them shoes she had on. The sky is big over Dartmoor, and once the road disappears, you're on your own. There are paths of course, but too many of them, so it's fairly easy to get lost. Luckily Bill knew the terrain well – so we kept close by him.

The further onto the moor we went, the wetter and more heavy going it got. I let Lydia hold on tight to me, and I liked that. I think she did too. We got five rabbits in all, the dogs bringing them back to us still alive. Those that were too small, we threw in the hedge, the others, we slit their throats. Lydia didn't like that much.

When we got back into the car, the Jack Russell jumped back onto

Lydia's lap and was sick all over her. By the end of the day, she looked like she'd lost a fight, badly. I was quite certain she'd never want to see me again but I was wrong. My charm had shone through.

She did of course ask questions about how I made my money and what I did for a living. I told her I was a welder, that I'd been to night school to get my qualifications. This impressed her, and my pimped-up Hillman Minx did the rest.

Four weeks after I met her, I asked her to marry me. Well that's not true actually. I asked her how much it would cost to marry her, and a few months later we threw an engagement party.

In between time, we'd gone for a weekend break to Challaborough Beach with Chrissie and his wife, Gayle. Challaborough is a sea of caravans that throughout the summer are taken over by the council house people from Plymouth. We used to go there as kids. For a lot of Plymouthians, Challaborough was the last outpost of their world – they never ventured further than that, ever. That wasn't me. Anyway, we only went there for a weekend away, staying in someone's caravan and getting some much-needed fresh air away from the grime and grubbiness of the city. Perhaps it was boredom, wanting to spice things up a bit – no matter – Gayle let slip to Lydia that her blue-eyed lover boy had never been near a night school to learn welding. She told her my expertise had all been learned in prison. Actually, I'd taught myself, but that's another story.

So Lydia had it out with me. I told her everything. And she was fine with it. She asked me to pack it all in and go straight, and I think I might have mumbled something that sounded like yes, but it wasn't a "yes" really. I had neither the intention nor the wherewithal to go straight. I'd have starved to death.

In the weeks after our first meeting, we went out a lot, mostly to the Camel's Head. I was on the run from the police for much of that time, and things got so hot that Lydia had to put me up in her brother's flat in Devonport so I wouldn't get nicked.

Lydia's Irish father took a while before he caught on to what I was up to. To be fair, he'd been doubtful from day one.

I first met him when I went round her house to call for her. I'd got used to calling her Nelly and so had no idea what her real name was. I rang the doorbell, and before anyone could answer it, I saw her dad pop his head round the back gate, He was in overalls, gardening.

"What do you want?"

"Errmm... I've come to see your daughter."

"Which one? I've got four."

"Mmm... Nelly? Ellie? Tellie?"

"There's no Nelly lives here. Wrong house, son."

I started to walk away.

"Do you mean our Lydia?"

"That's the one," I said.

He looked at me sideways. Not a great start.

Lydia

I was shy around boys and didn't put myself out there, not like some. My parents were the first for each other, so they were my role models.

The night I met David I'd only just finished a relationship. From that first meeting, we spent all our time together, day and night. Not all night. On our first day out together, we went rabbiting, which I had never done before. That night, we went babysitting for his brother. Another night, we went over to his mum's house. And another, down the Submarine. We rubbed along nicely together. Then on the fifth day it all got a bit out of hand – it was an accident really.

It was late, after the pubs had closed. We'd parked up outside our house and were just sitting in the car, talking. We'd sat and talked at the end of every night, ever since I'd met him. On this night, I looked up at our house to see my father looking out at us, a curtain twitching.

"Shall we go somewhere more private, David?"

I didn't tell him I'd seen my dad at the window – so David took the request for a change of venue as a green light. Of course, I could never tell my dad how big a part he'd played in all this.

I felt so bad the next day. As much as I liked David, I had to finish it with him. I couldn't bear the shame of it. All this made perfect sense to me but not to him of course. I felt like a slapper and I figured it was all his fault. I wasn't and never had been that kind of woman – I hadn't been brought up to behave like that.

Two days later we were all over each other again. We were eighteen years old.

I'd never risked smoking a cigarette before I met David, but within weeks of falling in love, I was on joints and snorting speed like the rest of them. We had a great time. David took me out for steak dinners and bought me clothes, and we were never short of a few bob to spend down the Submarine. The police were a constant threat, of course, but he didn't seem to pay much attention to them – I let him hide out in my brother's flat because they were after him for something. I knew what I was getting myself into and I didn't care. I loved him. My father on the other hand knew very little about what he got up to, and it stayed that way for some time.

David

I kept my secrets safe from Lydia's dad for about six months, until the day they were writ large in some detail in the *Evening Herald*. I'd been charged with burglary and assaulting a police officer. So then he began to look out for me. I had my own regular column in there for a while.

Lydia says that her father liked me but didn't like what I did for a living. He'd have coped with the embarrassment and shame better had he been able to contain it, but that ambition was thwarted on the day they buried his father-in-law, Lydia's grandfather.

There were quite a few guests at the wake, held back at the house after the funeral. Lydia's mum and dad had pushed the boat out, showing off with roast beef *and* ham on the bone. I was behaving myself, for Lydia's sake. Being quiet. Helpful. Passing out plates, that kind of thing. There were some uninvited guests to deal with as well. I noticed them first. The regional crime squad had turned up to look for me. I spotted them through the window. I'd seen something move in the hedge. So I took a closer look and found two CID officers staring back at me. I legged it. Lydia and her mum and some of her aunties and uncles were standing in the dining room, in my way, like a set of ten pins, arranged in a circle, talking. I knocked quite a few of them over on my way out. The police chased after me, up and over fences, across fields and through the back alleys of Swilly. They didn't catch me and none of Lydia's relatives admitted ever having seen me, which was kind of them, considering. Suffice to say, Lydia's father wasn't warming to me.

Lydia found the engagement ring she wanted in her sister's catalogue. I considered this a waste of money really, given my brother Stephen was one of the best jewellery thieves in the country. But she said the ring had to be straight or she wouldn't wear it. I kind of understood and respected her for taking a stand. It's a ring she still wears today.

***

The regional crime squad did finally catch up with me. I'd broken into a house in Sidmouth, a coastal town for rich retirees. Unbeknownst to me, it had been fitted with a silent alarm. I didn't stand a chance. They were outside the house before I knew they'd even arrived. They put me on remand in Exeter YP – prison for youths under twenty-one years of age. So this is where I was when Lydia was trying to organise our wedding.

Exeter is a city prison, Victorian and just a stone's throw away from Debenhams and Marks & Spencer. As they escorted me from reception into the prison proper, I could hear freedom fading into the distance. And sheep. I remember hearing sheep.

In the reception area, a large extended cell, they'd given me a brown uniform to wear, and shoes, an itchy blanket and a bed pack. As they walked me through to the landings, I was assaulted by all kinds of smells – BO, school dinners, and the slow creep of a musty stuffy odour coming off my new prison outfit. All of this was topped off with the reek of bleach and industrial cleaning solutions. They undid my cell door and I walked into my new home. My cellmate was a man called Harry Chown, a well-known local criminal with the gift of the gab and a sense of humour. I relaxed. It could've been a lot worse.

Most of the prisoners in Exeter were local, and so my family reputation cushioned me from the usual "settling in" trouble. I could enjoy the kind of respect lots of older men could never hope to command. I felt as comfortable and confident as the screws. This remand experience was an inconvenience really – certainly nothing to sweat about. I had every hope of getting off once my case went to court.

Life was a lot easier then on remand. Rather than get Lydia into trouble, I used to organise visits for prisoners who didn't have anyone else to visit them. This served two purposes. They got to meet someone from the outside to break up the monotony of the prison experience and I got a regular supply of drugs to smoke and money to spend on tobacco and whatnot. I was no druggy. I enjoyed a bit of blow and I took speed fairly regularly, but these were incidental to my life, not central to it. Inside prison and out, I only ever used drugs to take the edge off things.

Knowing Lydia was on the outside waiting for me did change how I experienced prison. I had someone else to think about now whilst I was in there, and visits to look forward to.

She wasn't pregnant. Our desire to marry quickly was a reflection of the intensity of the feelings we had for one another. We *knew* we were meant to be together. Even though I was in prison, Lydia just got stuck into the wedding preparations. To get the bans read, the vicar insisted on seeing me. He kept making appointments and Lydia kept making up excuses as to why I couldn't attend them, hoping I'd get bail soon enough, but I never did and so she had to tell him where I was in the end. Her parents weren't chuffed either, it has to be said. The idea of marrying their daughter off, in a prison chapel, wasn't what they'd had in mind. Something had to be done.

Lydia made it very clear she didn't want to spend the rest of her life prison visiting, not least because she was putting in an application to become a policewoman. I hadn't really considered how her choice of career might impact on my own. She had. She wanted me to consider a different kind of life after we were married. This is what we talked about when she came to visit me. She talked and I ate. She brought me chicken and cans of Super Tenants. Those were the days.

Reassured I had her best interests at heart, she arranged for the vicar to come and see me in prison. He stands out like a cardboard cut-out in my mind, for he was a hippy vicar with hair down his back and a long beard that snaked down past his chest. I'd never paid any mind to God or vicars in all my short life and so I can't recollect very much of what we talked about. Like me though, he wanted to see me released so I could attend my own wedding. Only a judge could grant me this freedom, a judge with the capacity to sympathise with my plight. Well, I'd already had quite a few bail hearings and I hadn't yet come across such a judge and doubted there was one.

Even my own brief told me, "You've got no chance of bail, and so I'm not going to ask for it." I ignored his advice and applied for it without him, which didn't go down well. On my final bail application, the vicar showed up in court. He sat at the back. My brief explained to the judge that he was there to substantiate my plea for freedom on the grounds of matrimonial imperative. But then he added, "However, your honour, it would not surprise me in the least if this man of the cloth had not been put up to the job by a member of the Hill family. I wouldn't put it past them." Luckily the judge ignored him and gave me bail, providing I agreed to sign on at the police station twice a day, every day, and be in off the streets by nine, every night, including my wedding night.

It was a big wedding. We had eleven bridesmaids. We hired a video cameraman to film it all, and a proper photographer, a really expensive one. We never paid him. We had family come down from Liverpool and from Ireland, from all over. We hired suits that never got taken back. Our Stephen was my best man. Even Lydia's dad rose to the occasion and gave a speech to give everyone the impression that he was *for* the marriage when I knew how dead against it he was. He escorted Lydia to the church in the wedding car, as was custom. As was not the custom, he spent that whole journey trying to talk his daughter out of the marriage. "You can stop it now. Right here. We can go home and forget all about it." She didn't take a blind bit of notice. She felt the same way about me as I did her.

A great day, that was. My mum was proud, I could tell. She didn't say much. She had to be dragged into the frame to have her picture taken, but she was filled with happiness for us both, and so was I. That night I signed on at the police station and stuck to my curfew, I was in by nine.

***

A couple of weeks later they banged me up for six months. When I came out, I went on the rampage. Driving.

I improved my driving skills learning the hard way, driving as fast as I could in stolen Vauxhall Novas, hired Nissan Bluebirds, borrowed Granadas and occasionally vehicles I purchased as and when I felt a need to. I drove a Ford Granada with five mates in the car and five police cars chasing me up Plymouth's new Parkway and then off it, to Swilly where I lived. It was a good few miles anyhow, and they didn't catch me. I always loved that – beating them at their own game.

***

When Lydia told me she was pregnant, I felt as any man does, I suppose, a sense of triumph on the one hand but also an acceptance that this is how life is and how it should be – how life is meant to be. When she told me she'd lost the baby, I carried on as usual.

***

I drove with passion, being chased, handling stolen goods or simply showing off to my mates. I was like a reckless child, driving for the hell of it, wanting to see what would happen if I drove as fast as I could, till... I crashed. Wanting to have that experience. Being that stupid. One day, I hired a Nissan Bluebird, a mile on its clock, to take the lads up to Exeter for a drink and a couple of burglaries en route. We got chased by the police. I drove so fast to lose them. I lost them all right and I lost grip. I flipped the car onto its roof. It slid down the road and just missed a ditch, and when it stopped careering, we all clambered out and ran off. None of us were hurt or caught. We had to split up, mind, and nick two more cars to get home again.

As I remember these days now, they come back to me in a blur of speed, a life rushed, the memories hurtling past me like the images you see through a car window when you're travelling at a hundred miles an hour. Some part of me believed the car was me – not just a means of transport, but a way of being, an extension of my body. Perhaps being attached to equipment for most of my formative years – a girdle and crutches – allowed me to feel psychologically secure enough to place trust in machinery as a means of transport. Certainly, I felt just as at home in a motor car as I did in a pair of trousers.

That's not to say I didn't come unstuck now and again. I'm ashamed to remember an evening when I was out and about, driving my own car and sober for a change, though without insurance. I was on the rob, alone, equipped with gloves, torch and screwdriver. And I was listening to Peter Tosh's "Legalise Marijuana", recalling my time in the Atkinson

Unit when I'd first heard it. I remembered playing it on my new Walkman, wearing headphones, fully plunged into the mood of the music, swaying about and all the rest of it – until I saw Frank, one of the prison warders cum tutors, outside my room, looking in on me, laughing. I was swaying about to Tosh again, but in a car driving fast down a dark narrow lane en route to a country house with promise, spotted earlier that day on our way home from another robbery. The "give way" sign was hidden by bushes, and I didn't see the marks on the road because I was reliving that feeling of joy, cocooned by sound, totally immersed in a piece of music that had had a profound impact on me – and I was only just then realising that fact. Reliving that sense of immersion was great, but this time I was hearing it as a free man, in a car, in complete control of my own destiny. Well, I was up until I hit a car head-on at a junction. What a smash. The other driver didn't budge. There was just silence. No noise. I jumped out to investigate. I found a very old lady slumped over her steering wheel. Her head was cut and she was bleeding heavily. I asked her if she was OK.

"I'm all right," she said, in a proper posh English accent. "I'm all right," she repeated.

"Good," I said. "Well then, I'll see yer later!"

And off I went. I ran away across the fields so the cops couldn't pick me up.

Like I said, I'm not proud.

One day, Tony and me burgled a house and actually found a car in the drive with the keys still in it. We drove it home through country lanes, fast, and then we found ourselves behind a car full of old people. I understood old people had to walk slowly if they were infirm, but I couldn't forgive any failure to make use of the accelerator, especially when I was stuck behind them, clearly in a hurry, trying to get past. So I rammed them. Hard. When the road widened, they did their best to get out of my way, but I rammed them again anyway, as punishment for winding me up in the first place. I hoped to encourage them to pay more attention next time. When we got close to our house, I did ninety miles an hour through the back alleys, purposely crashing the car into the walls on either side, just as I'd seen them do it on the telly. Me and Tony... Bad Steve... Martin... whoever I was with, I played at being Swilly's *Starsky and Hutch*. No journey was complete without a screech. I did not feel fear. I did not smell it. I would not give it house room.

I was a menace. I put my mates through so many near misses I can't think why they came out with me. We'd fly over humps and bumps doing fishtails, flips and rolls, and then go merrily on our way as if nothing had happened. I hated slow drivers, but worse than them, were stationary cars that meant I had to "stop". I liked to fly, and anything that got in my way – an old man getting into his car, lifting his little leg up to climb in – became a target, not an obstacle. On that occasion I only took the car door off its hinges. A few seconds earlier, it would have been his leg.

That was a near miss. There *were* hits as well. Head-on. There have been plenty of times when I've hit someone's vehicle and had to drive straight to Kevin Cooper's for a respray before the police came knocking, which they always did. It's a wonder I'm still alive, but it's an even bigger surprise to come out of that period of my life without having killed several if not lots of innocent people.

When Lydia told me she'd lost another baby, I felt nothing. I felt nothing because I was twenty-one years old and numb all over.

CHAPTER 10

Driving through Europe was less risky than in England. With police computers still yet to be invented, foreigners like us were hard to keep tabs on. And burgling was easier too. You could almost feel sorry for these Europeans – they were so lax with their security. Unlike in England, they still trusted one another. We used to stroll in and out of their offices and shops and take whatever was on offer. Money off desks. Handbags slung over office chairs. Drawers full of money. Stock piled high waiting to be stacked on shelves. We actually called these jobs "walk-ins" and when I say "we", I don't just mean my friends and I. Walk-ins were part and parcel of a villain's lifestyle back then. Half the young lads from Swilly, and a good proportion of the lads I got banged up with, had spent at least some time taking advantage of the good nature of our friends on the continent. Plymouth boys were particularly keen on this form of income, and perhaps, since our city has a history of sending adventurers out into the world for the purpose of plunder, we were only doing as Drake had done, albeit with rather more limited ambitions.

These trips were less an adventure and more like a job. Stephen, my brother, had been robbing Europe for years. He'd always concentrated his efforts on jewellery shops, flying into Zurich for the sole purpose of robbing as many diamonds from its city's jewellers as he could lay his hands on. He would enter a jeweller's shop, ask to see a tray of rings, and, by sleight of hand and distraction, remove the best ones off the tray and remove himself from the shop before the assistant had a chance to work out they'd been robbed. When they did finally realise, he was already taking a seat in the next shop, asking for a glass of water and suchlike. Our Stephen had perfected his act to the point of genius. He was a magician. You couldn't see him at it, even with a camera trained on him – I've watched CCTV recordings of my brother in action – and you can't see the trick, he's that quick. He'd do as many shops as he could fit into a day, then fly home again.

Stephen lifted a diamond worth eighty thousand pounds once and sold it in England for forty. He lived a merry-go-round life of easy come, easy go financing. He squandered his earnings liberally, getting drunk often, giving presents generously. As soon as his pockets were empty, he went back to work again. He gave his money to anyone who needed it, not least his children, whom he idolised, doted on and provided for as best he could and for as long as he could.

Lydia didn't like Stephen, and with good reason. Anyone could find all kinds of fault with him, and without much effort – he was short tempered, badly in need of some good manners, and quick... quick to move and very quick to violence. I've been in some pretty bloody scrapes with him. He is single-minded. He lives by the sword. He can start a fight with two chairs in an empty room. One of my worst experiences fighting with him was bloody, very bloody. We were drinking in the General More pub in Stonehouse when two girls came by and asked to speak to Stephen.

"Can you get us my MOT off these blokes – they won't give it to me. They've done the work and all but won't hand it over. We're at our wits' end."

Steve, always being generous to women, obliged, got off his stool and went to leave.

"Hang on," I said. "I'm coming with you."

"No. No need," he said. "I'll do this on my own."

"I'm coming with you." I left my beer and followed him and the girls out. "I'm driving."

So off we went. I drove like a fiend. Stephen sat next to me. The two girls were in the back. When we got to the house, Stephen got out and knocked on the man's door. The bloke came out and they started arguing in the street. Then fighting. Just then, another car drew up. Turned out to be the man's brother. He piled in, so I jumped out of the car and was on him. Kicking him. He got hold of my foot and threw me to the ground. I felt blood pouring from my head. Stephen got him off me, and then the two men ran towards the house and we went after them. I caught one of them – and using a broom I picked up from the front path, I started hitting him with the handle. Every time I hit him it snapped, making it smaller and easier to wield, until I was left with just a pointed spear. So I stabbed him with that a few times before he managed to get away from me again. He ran into the house, down the hall and into the kitchen. I pushed at the door but couldn't open it – but Stephen managed a big push and got in there. They were waiting for him. They shut the door behind him and laid into him. They had a big metal bar in there and they whacked him with it. I tried my best to get in there but they were up against the door preventing me. I found some oven cleaner spray in a cupboard near the door, and so when the door partially opened as I pushed it, I sprayed the guy's face through the gap in the door. Then I ran round the back of the house to see if I could get in round the back. I found a big toolbox and chucked it right at them, through the window. Then I picked up two ball hammers that had been in it and used these to get in through the rear door to the kitchen. With a ball hammer in each hand I smashed at the glass, some of it embedding itself inside my hand. I went at the door like a machine, just smashing my way through – there was no stopping me and they knew it. The door gave way like plywood. Meanwhile, Stephen was still bleeding profusely in the kitchen. When I got through, I could see he had a huge gash down the side of his head. There was so much blood. The kitchen was streaked in it. They'd got out of there, the men, through another door into the lounge, where I could hear a woman crying with fear. Now I began to smash my way through the lounge door with the ball hammer, just like Jack Nicholson in *The Shining*. When I finally got through, I found the two men and the woman quivering in the corner of the lounge, their faces white, as if their blood had already been spilt.

"We'll be back," we said. "So don't think you've got away with it."

I put Stephen in the car and took him straight up to the hospital. The two blokes followed us up there within the hour – clutching the MOT certificate. They moved out of the house the next day.

Whilst our Stephen would go out every day and fight, he was a loyal brother and a loving, generous father who would part with his last pound if it meant improving the fortunes of his offspring. Because he's my brother, I love him. And I, more than most, can and do cope with his fits and starts and unacceptable behaviour.

***

Stephen used to have a good relationship with a man called Vince Harris who lived on the Leidseplein in Amsterdam, and the first time I went to Holland I headed straight for Harris's apartment, driving a red B-reg Ford Fiesta. Before I left England, I spent the last of my English cash eating at an Indian restaurant in Dover. I was hungry in more ways than one. The whole point of the trip was to get easy money, quickly, burgling, using Stephen's mate Vince as a fence to liquidate my ill-gotten assets before returning home, loaded.

I didn't rest much en route or on the ferry, so by the time I got into Holland I was so tired my peripheral vision had gone. I had to stop in a lay-by and rest. I was quite close to Amsterdam but not near enough to risk any more driving. When I woke up, my hazards were flashing, and for a millisecond – but long enough – I thought I was still driving, and I freaked, grabbing hold of the steering wheel to take control of the vehicle. That shook me up a bit.

All the houses in Amsterdam look the same, and so it was hard work finding Vince's flat, though I'd memorised his address by heart. I got there eventually, and so Vince and I went out to the Bulldog (a large pub full of lowlife Brit kids getting high on the novelty of getting high without getting arrested) immediately, to catch up, drink beer and smoke some grass.

Vince Harris was an archetypal low-rent villain with a blond feather cut, a face like a scrunched-up bag of crisps and a weaselly expression that he wore all the time to indicate an evident dislike of his immediate surroundings – no matter where he was or who was with him. He was a wrong'un. I wouldn't have trusted him with the change from a fag machine had we not been wishing to take advantage of his town centre accommodation.

After getting off my face with him, I couldn't remember where I'd parked the car and so I had to borrow money off Vince and stomach the cost of getting a clamp removed. I felt like I was going down a plughole fast. I had to get to work.

Vince was easy enough to get along with, but a bit of a liability, had a mouth on him. He'd grass you up before catching a cold for you. He at least helped me find some houses to burgle, and my first one, a maisonette, had a little stream running in front of it with a small bridge over it. I went and knocked and waited, and once I was sure there was no one in, I went round the back and broke a window. I was halfway through the rooms when I heard something. A little boy talking. Then a car pulled up outside. I only just managed to get out of the house before they got in. Close call.

I got into another house, a large corner house all on its own, not as big as the maisonette and difficult to break into. I had to really bash the window. I went straight for the bedroom – like English people, the Dutch kept their jewels in boxes on the dressing table. I got a Hunter watch, diamond rings and a Dutch sovereign. I kept the sovereign and attached it to a chain which I wore round my neck and which was removed from me by the customs police on my return home.

"Where do you get this then, eh?"

I'd sold the rest of my haul on to Vince, and for a price far in excess of what I could have expected for similar jobs here in England. This was partly due to the fact that European gold is of a higher quality than English. They sell a minimum 14 carats whereas the English go down to 8. The other big plus robbing houses on the continent rather than at home is that the people over there had more to rob, a lot more. They had houses worth breaking into. Good-quality jewellery and lots of gold, mostly 18–22 carats. The other draw was Vince himself. Whilst he needed watching, you couldn't odds the fact that he was a good fence, converting our ill-gotten gains to cash rapidly, albeit we had to have a barney on the rate every time. I could burgle one house for the price of two in Holland, returning home with a big bag of cash and leaving no trail of evidence behind me.

My Dutch sovereign was 22 carat gold, and whilst the customs knew I'd probably robbed it, as I've pointed out before, gold in classic formats like chains and coins is untraceable to any specific person or location. And so they couldn't pin a job on me. Not that they ever gave up trying.

On the way back from my first foreign foray, I met two young girls on the ferry and bought them a drink in the bar. They were funny. And skint. They'd been offered a lift home by some bloke who they didn't feel comfortable with – they were hiding from him. When I clocked him, I could see why. I'm a generous man at heart – so if I can do you a favour, I will. Back then, not many people knew this about me and so I didn't get to help out that many people, to be honest. But when I was asked, I always felt a satisfying flush of importance and responsibility when and if I was able to oblige. And if I was thanked properly for something I'd done, the glow I felt inside... well you can't buy that stuff in a shop. It was valuable to me.

The next time I went to Holland, I travelled with Stephen, and again we planned to stay in Vince's flat. Stephen was after more diamonds, and me, more burglaries, this time on housing estates on the edge of the city. In the event, neither of us were very successful. We only managed a few small jobs each. Vince sold our hauls quickly, albeit at top rent – but this meant we were able to return to England risk-free and with a bit of cash in our pockets. On this occasion, we returned via Dover. We weren't entirely clean as we'd bought a couple of ounces of speed for our personal use and were therefore carrying – we weren't drug dealers back then though.

I was driving a hired red Vauxhall Nova 1200 B-reg, a brand new one, bright red. We got through customs at Dover all fine, tickety-boo, or so we thought. It wasn't until we got onto the motorway that we realised we had company. Whilst we weren't drug dealers, the speed was already bagged up into parcels, so it looked very much like we were. I didn't want to get locked up on a misunderstanding, so I made a run for it. Stephen, like me, immediately assumed that Vince had grassed us up – probably to get himself out of trouble, which was kind of how he operated. We would later discover this wasn't the case. Customs had run a check on Stephen's passport number after we'd passed through immigration and decided to take their chances.

I, likewise, thought I'd take mine. I took the next slip road off the motorway and we soon had another police car on our tail. So I took them for a ninety mile per hour scenic ride up and down the lanes of Kent's countryside. I'd have gone faster had the car been able to. We skirted round bends, drove straight through red lights and even over a couple of train crossings, as I remember. I was determined they wouldn't get to me whilst we still had bags of speed in the car. Stephen was offloading the powder into the wind, a bag at a time. It took ten miles of the chase to get rid of all the bags. Then I stopped the car and got out.

At least five police cars stopped and all the coppers jumped out. Four of them came over. One of them captured Stephen and grabbed hold of him by the neck. Another two coppers held onto me, whilst the last, the biggest, laid into me. Seriously. He punched and kicked me till I fell senseless to the floor. He kicked my head in and didn't stop till the other coppers restrained him.

It had been a good car chase. Even though they had much faster vehicles than my Vauxhall Nova, even though they had God on their side, they still couldn't catch me. If I hadn't stopped, they'd have had to call for more backup and roadblocks to stop me. They looked foolish, and that's one thing the police can't stomach. Not in public.

Eventually they took us to a police station in Ashford. News had preceded us. The custody sergeant didn't even try to hide his admiration for my driving skills.

"In a Vauxhall Nova! For ten miles. Unbelievable. You're in the wrong job, mate. You should be a rally driver."

Delighted as I was by this unusual gift of a compliment from a policeman, I couldn't join in this conversation because I couldn't open my mouth – my jaw didn't work any more. I tried to point this out to them, both before and during the subsequent interview, but they decided to crack on anyhow. Eventually one of them sussed that I wasn't talking because I couldn't talk. I was in desperate need of a doctor.

They sent me to the hospital in a police car but without an escort, and they allowed our Stephen to come with me. At the hospital, X-rays revealed my jaw to be broken in three places. The police turned up shortly afterwards and had words with the doctor, words I couldn't hear. The police then came to my bed to see me. The doctors wanted to wire my mouth up there and then – they advised me to stay and be admitted so I could have the work done immediately. The police, realising the extent and import of their error, offered me a deal, which I refused. I was going to make them pay. I was going to have my day in court, I told them. So I left the hospital and set off for Plymouth with a broken jaw and a determination to prosecute – a determination that would eclipse their efforts to make my life a misery.

The jaw was broken three times on the line of my wisdom teeth, so the gums had to be cut top and bottom and all four embedded wisdom teeth removed. They pulled the teeth out under general anaesthetic in an operating theatre, and afterwards the pain was tremendous. I've never felt pain like it. My head swelled and the morphine rush was short-lived. Because my mates came into the ward bearing drink and drugs, and not very discretely, the nurses decided to limit my analgesic, so I was in a lot more pain than I needed to be. I was left in excruciating pain all day and all night and all the next day too.

I vowed the next time a copper came near me I'd do to him what they'd done to me. This as well as a prosecution, not instead of. If they came to arrest me, I wouldn't go quietly. And of course, it didn't take too long for just such an opportunity to present itself.

***

I asked my solicitor Antony Daniels to take on my case against the police. He refused. I was surprised. He said he wouldn't serve me any more on account of the fact he'd caught Bad Steve red-handed robbing his house in the middle of the night. He must have thought I'd had a hand in it – I hadn't. Had Bad Steve done his research and known whose house it was, I feel sure he'd have left well alone. Bad Steve didn't work solo very often and so he wasn't very pro-active in planning and executing burglaries at his own behest. I can only assume he must have been a bit short that week and had to go out robbing to get funds in.

Whilst Antony Daniels was hard-faced and knew the law for the nasty piece of bendy plastic that it is, Michael Rowe was a gentleman's solicitor and the person I eventually briefed to represent me in my fight against the police. Rowe was soft-voiced and always tried hard to appeal to the better nature of judges rather than test (as in irritate) their intellect, as Daniels was so fond of doing. Rowe assured me that we'd win. But that wasn't enough for me. An eye for an eye – a jawbone for a jawbone – only then would I feel as if justice had truly been served.

Lydia

I just let him get on with it. I would ask for help from time to time, if and when he was home, but I never nagged him or tried to change him. I put up with the crime, the travel, the danger he got into, because I loved him. I enjoyed the spoils as well of course, but they didn't mean so much to me. I've never been motivated by money and I certainly wouldn't have encouraged him to endanger himself or his freedom just so we could have some. I knew what I'd married into, so I couldn't complain it wasn't perfect, could I?

I don't know if he knew just how much it hurt to keep miscarrying kids. I felt it was all my fault, that I must have done something wrong. Physically there was a problem, that was for sure. David wanted a child and I felt guilty because I appeared to be incapable of giving him one. All our friends and family – they were having babies, no problems at all. Because my mum had had the same trouble, I figured it must be something that ran in the family.

The crime. The police raids. Jail. Being alone when he went off to Europe. I didn't care what he was getting up to. I took all that in my stride. I knew that he loved me; that was important. Not being able to carry his child full term – that was almost too much to bear.

All I'd ever wanted was to be a mother, and yet I lost three babies within twelve months of us being married. For six of those months,

David was in prison. He'd go for a night out and not come back for months or weeks on end. One time, it took him two years to find his way home again. I think if I'd had a child to look after I could have borne his absence more gracefully. But I was losing babies not bearing them. I was waking up to find my bed soaked in blood, and that took something away from me, out of me. He knew I was suffering. But he couldn't fix it. This was a problem he couldn't burgle his way out of. Before I got pregnant again, we were sent to see a consultant.

"Well, Mr and Mrs Hill. We've done our tests and it's bad news I'm afraid." He could hardly look us in the eye. Keeping his distance so not to feel anything.

David and me were well used to bad news, but I just couldn't bear to think we'd never have kids.

"It seems doubtful you'll ever be able to carry a child full term. So I'm going to recommend you attend a clinic for some genetic counselling."

David wouldn't wear it. Even though he'd spent all that time in hospital as a kid, perhaps because he had, he was so out of his comfort zone being back there at the mercy of doctors. The jargon got to him. Got to me too. They don't want to give you support – they want to scare you.

"If you ever do manage to go full term, it's ninety-nine per cent certain the child will have Down's syndrome. Now whether you choose to go ahead with those kinds of odds is not a decision to take lightly. Which is why I'm suggesting you undertake genetic counselling so you can fully explore the many and varied consequences of proceeding and/or not proceeding with your plans for a family."

What kind of decision was that to make?

"I want a baby."

"Then we'll keep on trying," said David.

My dad was devastated. He wanted the family to club together to pay the fees for IVF. He would have sold everything, he told me, the house, the lot, if he thought he could get me a baby. *Me* a baby, not David. My dad loved us, his blood, his kin, his anchor in life. He couldn't look on and see me so unhappy. When push came to shove, he had no mind for principles – he just threw the rule book out the window. When one of my sisters got pregnant at sixteen, he told her (like me) that she had choices. She didn't have to marry the no-mark who knocked her up.

She could live under his roof, as family. But the lad was forced to marry her by his parents anyway. It wasn't much of a marriage, because he slept around like a dog. They got divorced years ago.

We were living in Whitleigh, a housing estate on the outskirts of the city, en route to Dartmoor. We had our own flat. I'd given up working in the fish market. I worked in Boots for a while as well but I didn't like it there so much. The fish market wasn't exactly a ball but I really liked the other women there – I liked being with friends all day. Better than being at home without any kids to look after. By the time David came home from his last trip to Holland I'd lost another baby, the fourth.

I felt like I was fading away, so the next time David went abroad, he took me with him. We travelled through several countries at full speed. He only stopped to do walk-ins. He broke my nose in Holland doing an emergency stop. I didn't complain then. I'm not a doormat, I'm not. I just don't see the point of causing trouble and grief if there's no solution. It was an accident, that was all.

If David shared anything of my character it was a need to find fast solutions to problems that were fixable. I wanted a baby. I didn't care if it had Down's syndrome, whether it was big, small, blind or deaf. I just wanted a family of my own. I could have had anything else in the world – a new car, a new house, constant travelling, clothes to fit a princess, all of these were in my gift – and I know David would have worked night and day to give them to me, had I made the tiniest gesture to suggest such things would make me happy – but I never did. No matter how hard he worked, or how clever he was, he couldn't conjure up babies that didn't want to be born. The last miscarriage was twins. I found it so much harder to say goodbye to them – harder than all the others put together.

David

I carried on with my international business trips, sometimes in the company of Gary Rankin, the sock seller. We went to Amsterdam and met up with some other friends with a plan to scour whole neighbourhoods of shops and offices doing walk-ins. We cleaned up. I went abroad again with Derek, this time to Antwerp. We did OK till a shop burglary went wrong on us. There were four of us. It was a clothes shop. Someone had sighted us and called the police. They came at us from all directions and we ran off. Everyone got caught but me. I hid away. I waited three hours before risking any movement. I went to collect the car. It was a hire car. They were waiting for me.

Loads of police cars – too many to count – chased me through the high streets of Antwerp in the dark. I didn't know where I was going but they did. Eventually they surrounded me. I was forced out the car and told to put my hands up. They put a gun to my head, which, being as used to British cops as I was, I found quite disconcerting. They took me to their police station and locked me in a cell. I shared the cell with a mouse that night. Guns aside, the Antwerp police were very genial. Kind. Polite. Civil. No hard feelings, they decided to ship us all back to England the following day. They walked us onto the boat in handcuffs, to embarrass us, I think. That worked. We didn't have a bean between us. We were forced to do walk-ins down in the cabins – we were all starving. As the people slept or got drunk in the bars, we robbed them blind and had a good trip home in the end.

Many of these trips merged into one another, we were back and forth so often. Another time, again with Derek, we went to Belgium to rob some jewellers' shops in Bruges. I'd grown up with Derek in

Grassendale Avenue and come to trust him. I enjoyed his company. He was an early balding man with uneven teeth and a passion for kick-boxing. He was a grafter really, not a thief. He was into landscape gardening when there was work. Like Bad Steve, he would come along as much for the ride as the company – and the buzz of course. We all loved the buzz. We'd sit in the Camel's Head, come up with an idea, then go rob and do. Holland. Belgium. Germany. France. One trip, end half of 1985, we went to Bruges for walk-ins and were particularly successful. This time we went to a toy shop and found a bag of cash on the table in the office upstairs. Four grands worth of florins in our pocket. Off we went. Sometimes we'd come back through Zeebrugge or we'd carry on with our journey through France. We'd be on the *Herald of Free Enterprise* more times than I care to remember – the scabbiest boat there was with a restaurant even I refused to eat in. Sometimes we'd come back via Roscoff directly to Plymouth.

A lot of shops attached a bell to their shop door to alert them to intruders. We found an easy way to insert a piece of plastic into the mechanism so the bell didn't ring. Then we'd go in and collect our haul and book ourselves into a posh hotel for the night. Some hotels weren't all they were cracked up to be. One night in Holland, it was boiling hot, and late at night, we finally stopped. We were forced to take a bed in the last hotel in town because everywhere else was booked up. When we went up to our room and turned the light on, a frenzy of forty thousand flies woke up and started dancing round the room – literally thousands of them. I got an aerosol of deodorant, lit a flame and torched them all. The ceiling turned black. When I woke in the morning, my bed was full of dead spiders and flies – crisp and dry. I rolled over and heard them crunch. I told the woman at breakfast that I'd been wrestling spiders all night – and that they'd had me by the neck and thrown me to the ground. She just laughed at me.

On one of these trips we went back to England via Zeebrugge and then straight to Hatton Garden. We sold our haul of jewellery for scrap, netting eight thousand pounds.

I did a few more jobs with Derek, and one in particular that nearly finished us. We got chased off the job at the very last minute and were on the run for ages. We had to bury the jewels in a forest. We sent a man called Matt, an ex-security guard, back to Belgium to dig all the jewels up again. He got to the jewels all right, but then went and dipped his hands in the bag. He'd pay for that later, and dear, that was for certain.

The last time I went abroad with Derek, we flew British Airways to Copenhagen for no other reason than I'd not been there before. I figured if it was no good we could drive down to Holland and do the usual. We hired a Ford Sierra car at the airport and drove through Denmark to Luxembourg. I kept my foot jammed on the accelerator all the way – not slowing down for anyone, as fast as the car would go, which, with the wind behind us, was about a hundred and five miles an hour them days, in a hire car. Much of the road was flanked by forest, mile after mile of it. We were driving through a forest when a reindeer jumped out at us. I'd normally try and steer around obstacles, but this was a huge moving object the size of a small building and with its own agenda. So I put my foot on the brake. Just as well I did. We saw every single spot on its neck and on its cheek – we got that close. That was a close one.

We'd planned to do walk-ins in the towns and cities en route, but after the deer jumped out on us, I lost my vim. I don't know what happened. I just didn't feel like going robbing. I couldn't bring myself to do it. There was no momentum. Derek was the same – or perhaps he was just following my lead. There was no energy in me. Overnight, it felt like I'd lost my bottle. I couldn't tell Derek how I really felt, but as I remember it now, I can say I was experiencing some kind of heartache. Something stirred deep within me and it pained me. We lost the car and instead got on a train in the south of France, heading back to Roscoff. I wanted to sail home for England. It was a long journey, heavy going, though my pockets were empty. I was clean all over. When I finally got back, Lydia looked ready to give birth – like she was going to burst. "No," she said. "I've another two months to go."

I had to brace myself then. What kind of kid would we get, if it did manage to make it to the finish line? What kind of kid did I deserve, in fact?

***

My brother Tony was perhaps the most reliable and dependable of the Hill family, but he didn't stand much chance of a normal life, given all his brothers above and below were wrong'uns. Our Maureen fared better, and miraculously, she turned out to be the kind of daughter any mother could wish for. Our Tony enjoyed a good rapport with everyone, but as I said earlier, especially so with the women. He had a young babyface, a bit like mine, but he was also blessed with a lot more hair than me. He could manage eye contact too, and well. He was dark, suave and swarthy. That said, he was quiet, resolute and not subject to unpredictable temper tantrums or violent outbursts. Being comparatively mild (if you stood him next to our Stephen), he did still have his moments. I once saw him take a chair leg to Jim, my mum's boyfriend. This was after he got told to buck his ideas up. "You're not my dad, so lay off!"

Tony wasn't exactly honest John, but he *was* the only brother of mine who managed to keep a job – for a while. But mindless work on conveyor belts at the Toshiba telly factory didn't stimulate him *that* much. Well, not enough to inspire him with ideas or aspirations to hang about waiting on a promotion. With career development opportunities at a minimum, he took a reality check and his last pay cheque and returned to the streets he knew and loved so well. He often went out on the rob with me and with others, but never to accumulate a reputation for himself or build an empire. His passion for designer clothes meant that if a proper job was out of the question, then a certain level of risk-taking was more of a necessity than a lifestyle choice. Like so many men on our estate engaged in nefarious activities, he was hardly in it for the glory either. Our Tony was good-looking, happy-go-lucky and up for any opportunity to earn. So he learned quickly that it was far easier and more satisfying to earn his money tax-free, out on the rob with the rest of us, enjoying flexible hours and the occasional bonus when we got lucky. It was the only way he could fund his favourite pastimes: dressing up and paying for expensive nights out with women. On 31st October 1986, not long after my return from Copenhagen, we were still living in a flat in Whitleigh. Lydia was eight months gone and still going.

Lydia

This pregnancy is the one I cared least about. For all the others, I'd rested, ate well, and protected myself and given way to any and every suggestion of the doctor. With this one, I just didn't care. When you've had five miscarriages, this is what it's like. I drank like a fish. I'm ashamed to say I snorted speed, smoked fags and had myself a great time. One night we went on a booze cruise up the Tamar to a pub in Calstock, a village in Cornwall. Whilst we were all getting bladdered downstairs in the pub, one of David's mates went upstairs to rob it and got caught, so then we all had to leave, sharpish. We ran. We ran over fields and through bushes, up hills and down ditches. I have never run so hard in my life because half the men of Calstock were after us. And my baby just put up with it. She lived through it.

It was 1986. Hallow'en. We were sitting in the Submarine pub. There was me David and Tony. And a load of mates sitting around. Tony was making me laugh. He kept going on about me being pregnant. I was huge. Tony was saying that because I was so tall and because David was so tall, they'd be pulling the baby out of me non-stop, forever, on and on and on... and he made hand gestures like he was pulling washing out of a tub. That was the last conversation I ever had with him.

We heard there was a party over at the General More pub in Stonehouse, so we drove over there in two cars. It promised to be a good night out, but Tony wanted to go back to the Submarine, probably to see a woman, I don't know. When David I got home that night, we went straight to bed, but we got woken up by Barry Turner who'd come to tell us that Tony had been run over.

I offered to drive because... because David was all over the place, but he wouldn't let me or anyone else drive him around. Never has, never will. It was a very solemn drive, but in a bright yellow Morris Marina. When we got to the hospital, he parked it round the back and put it right up close to the wall, as if he already knew there was a dead end approaching.

Steve Trimm was OK. Tony was not OK but in bed, connected to wires and drips. His eyes were closed, dead to the world. He was attached to a ventilator, his mum sitting by his side. She seemed almost transparent, so pale and wasted-looking the veins in her head all stood out. I couldn't look at her. I felt the most pregnant I'd ever felt in that room in that moment. As his mother relayed the events of the night before, as she'd understood them, I looked out of the window, down into a yard full of giant-sized dustbins.

Tony and Steve had left the Submarine at 11 pm and walked across the road towards their car – David's car. But then someone had called out Tony's name. Tony doubled back to go and speak to the person shouting after him. As he walked back, a car came round the corner too fast to brake in time. It slammed straight into Tony and knocked him down. Steve was just two feet away from joining him. Steve says it still makes him go cold to think of it.

They kept Tony alive for a couple of days, and on 2nd November 1986, they finally pulled the plug. His mother was devastated.

When we left the hospital, David told me to take his mum home. He just walked off and left me and his mother standing there. Things like that – David has to deal with trouble all on his own. He'll just go off and deal with it in his own way. After a couple of pints he ended up going to Channings Wood Prison to tell Stephen. Then he drove to Dartmoor prison to tell Martin. Tony was just twenty-five years old when he died.

We went to live with David's mum after that. We still had the flat at Whitleigh but David didn't want to leave his mum on her own. The other two sons were locked up and Maureen was married. His other sister still lived in South Africa.

David's mum was a very strong character. I suppose she had to be, bringing up six kids all on her own. She got carted off to police stations more times than we'd care to remember, handcuffed usually. Put in the back of police cars. But she stuck up for her kids. After Tony died, she said, "Right, six weeks of mourning and that's it." And that's exactly what she did. Like I said, a strong character. She worked non-stop. She had COPD and couldn't walk very far at all, but she'd get up and wash a plate if there was one sitting dirty looking at her. She was happy to be busy. And everything had to be just right. Everything was placed in exactly the same place. She hoovered at the same time every day. She laundered on the same days every week. She cut sandwiches into triangles and made sure they were all the same size. No matter what her boys got up to, she loved them. She loved all her kids and showed it. David would kiss and cuddle her to show his appreciation, but Martin never would. He showed no emotion towards her at all.

David

Like Dad being dead, our Tony will always be dead. Even now, I cannot think of Tony without a sadness, for so much was lost, *is* lost without him, his young vibrant spirit, my brother.

We were a close family and a pragmatic one, so we did get on with our lives afterwards, yes, and with heavy hearts, but we never lost our own spark for living. My mother needed comfort and space to grieve, and we all, and especially Aunty Jean, gave her both, as much as she could take from us. It was, I suppose, a long pause in a life that was otherwise filled with all kinds of music. The only sound to be heard was the knell, an echo of a dark note being hammered into the metal. We took up from that note and went on. And we still go on. The music doesn't ever stop.

You might think with our Tony being knocked down by a drunk driver I'd be more careful on the roads, more sympathetic to the vulnerability of pedestrians and other drivers in my midst. You might think that, but you'd be wrong. I didn't change my driving behaviour any. I still drove fast, drunk, and with no thought to the safety of others. On the contrary, I congratulated myself on being able to avert "accidents" by virtue of my quick thinking and navigational dexterity. Police chases, quick getaways, getting home in time for dinner – nothing stopped me driving at speed, illegally, with or without substances in my bloodstream. The car was an extension of my skin – a shell to protect me from the unpredictable. I was in charge of the car – no one could touch me in it.

***

One out, one in, as they say.

When you've been waiting so long for a child to arrive, full term, you do kind of want to be there when they finally make their way down the birth canal. Wasn't a pretty sight, that's for sure. It was the night of the 15th December 1986. Lydia and I were, by chance, together at her sister Valerie's house. Valerie had gone out to some Christmas shindig. We were babysitting, close and comfy, watching TV, a fire roaring. Then Lydia went into labour. Valerie had to leave her party early and come back so I could get Lydia up to the hospital. Sadly, all the doctors were also at a party that night, so when Lydia's labour turned all gnarly, there were very few professionals on hand to support her. They were called back from their celebrations and came into the birthing room mob-handed, and drunk. They stunk of alcohol.

Our child was doing her level best to stay put in her womb, resisting all pushes and pulls to release her. So they got the forceps out eventually. My poor wife – she had it rough all right. If the child wasn't already damaged, I knew that after this club-fisted attempt to bring her into the world, she most certainly would be now.

Our daughter Jade was finally born breathing, and to much relief all round. She was not Down's, and not injured in any way. She was just perfect in fact. I kissed her dirty little crusty head smeared with blood, smelling of us. I squeezed Lydia's hand and filled the silence with the very best of me. Tears fell down my cheeks for the first time in a long time. We were three, all one, close, all rejoicing. This was something special, certainly.

After a couple of days in hospital, we wrapped Jade up in white swaddling blankets and took her home to Whitleigh. We broke down on the way home, but hey-ho! Nothing could have dampened our rejoicing and our pleasure. No one could have been prouder than us.

My own mum was still grieving the loss of our Tony, and now as a dad I had some inkling – not much to be sure – but some inkling of the boundless love that flows from parent to child and so some indication of how that loss might feel should a child die on you. I was deeply attached to my daughter Jade instantaneously, and I always will be.

Lydia was born to be a mum. She must have known that. She'd lived through so many miscarriages, yet she'd been determined to continue with the mission in spite of all the risks being pointed out to us. She was a natural – which doesn't mean she was overly sentimental or obsessed. She was responsive, curious, happy, and importantly in her element. As a dad, I could not have been happier.

As a dad, it was now all the more important for me to get to work and bring home some bacon. I hired a D-reg Sierra and planned a series of raids to fill up the coffers as the list of requirements for baby and mother was as long as I had the time and energy needed to add to it. Sadly, on the first day of the hire (this was during the Christmas holidays, and it had been touch and go getting the car in the first place), whilst I was enjoying a quiet drink, some fool broke into the car through the back window. On the rob of course. Hoping to find Christmas pressies in the boot no doubt! This was highly inconvenient as I'd been planning to go out that very afternoon on a fairly serious job. I knew if I took the car back to the hire firm there'd be complications. No other cars to hire. Conversations with the police and the insurance company, not to mention a million forms to fill in – I was OK at signing my name, but writing full sentences and descriptions was a challenge I'd avoid at any cost. But I didn't want to miss an opportunity to make some easy money. I had stuff to buy now I was a father. Playpens, toys and clothes, a new bathroom to fix up and an old fireplace to rip out. Not to be deterred, I decided my best bet would be to find a similar car to mine and replace my back window with theirs. Not so difficult as you might think, by the way.

We drove around looking out for an identical make and model – there were three of us in the car. We found one fairly quickly, on Millbay Road in Plymouth. We parked up, got out of our car and set upon the rear window of a brand spanking new Sierra with a roll of wire and some pliers and other tools. We were so engrossed in our work we didn't notice the cop car pull up. The door slams alerted us. Two of them stood there, staring right at us. They had their *"It's our lucky day"* smirk turned on full. They wouldn't be smiling for long, was my first thought. This was the first opportunity I'd had to make good on my promise to batter the very next policeman who had the gall to try and arrest me. So it wasn't their lucky day after all.

No questions. No talking. I just laid right into them. Hammered them. The fight ended after I threw one on the floor and broke his arm. The other one hit me over the head with his truncheon and made a good job of it. The navy provost turned up then, so whilst the coppers were distracted, I took my chance and ran off. I had so much blood pouring out of my head I couldn't see where I was going. They all came after me. I ran down back streets, down Bath Street, onto the Octagon on Union Street and into the Kentucky Fried Chicken. I joined the queue. Tried to blend in. Not possible. My head was pumping blood. The assistants behind the counter took exception to the mess, as did the people I was in the queue with. I was causing too much commotion to hide away, and so the provost eventually found me and took me off to the naval hospital to put stitches in my head. I was confined to a room and could not, no matter how hard I tried, figure out a way to escape from there. They were all waiting for me outside.

They took me to Charles Cross Police Station, where, once again, even though *I'd* battered *them*, they tried to do a deal with me. The Kent police were still very keen for me to drop the charges. They would, they promised, charge me with a less serious offence.

"No deal. No way."

My last words on the matter. I hated them. I was going to have my day in court, no matter what it cost me.

They took to me to jail, to Exeter, on remand for two charges – firstly, for assaulting a police officer (no police officers were put on remand for assaulting me, mind), and secondly on a charge of reckless (but damn fine) driving relating to the police chase all around Kent.

In jail, I was to share a cell with a man called Jagga. On my arrival, he didn't move. And when he spoke, it was quietly.

"All right, mate."

"All right," I replied.

Nothing then for ages.

You never know if you're going to get a nutter or a know-all – both can have a very negative impact on your prison experience. By far the best shout is to end up alone. This was not to be.

Jagga was mixed race, but I don't know which nationalities had been combined to produce his dark skin and curly dark hair. He'd been raised in kids' homes, was knocked about a lot, he said. He certainly had more than his fair share of scarring across his face, hands and arms, but not so much to detract from his good looks. His presence was such you would forgive him errors of judgement that others could never get away with – white socks, for instance. He was a drug dealer, a proper one, not some lightweight off some council estate in Exeter or Plymouth. He'd been shipped out of a nick in Manchester and was, he admitted, a fish out of water. That was very true, but not in a bad way. Immediately we got on. He didn't talk nonsense. We both had the same aim – to make lots of money. We were interested in each other and so shared ideas and plotted new ways of achieving what was a shared vision – to do as little as possible for as much cash as we could get our hands on. He could play the guitar as well, which helped.

It turned out he had something far more valuable to offer than I could have dreamt of. He was part of a drugs network with contacts all over the world, the best of them home-grown and close to hand – one, Paul Massey, the kingpin of Moss Side at that time.

Paul Massey was a notorious villain who in later years would run for Mayor of Salford to stand up for the "people". He was unsuccessful in that but he was right about the fact that he'd get shot before he was allowed to die naturally. Years later, his funeral, which took place in Salford, would be attended by hundreds and hundreds of people who clearly had some respect for him. Back then, so did I. I wanted, in my own way, to be him – well to be as successful as him. But I rush on. At this point, I'm just making friends with one of Massey's men who nursed his own dream of becoming the next Mr Big, with all the fame and fortune such a title would bestow, albeit gotten illegally. After a couple of days in the cell with Jagga, I understood that dealing drugs would be, by some distance, the best and safest way to earn huge sums of money quickly.

Jagga's own income from his drugs activities was substantial, and his time in prison merely an opportunity to rest up and regroup; to consider different strategies and network dynamics; to make an even bigger killing once freedom had been granted. People often say that prisons are just universities of crime. I'm not so sure about that. Most of the convicts I met didn't offer me or anyone else much in the way of an education, criminal or otherwise. But there are, in any prison, always one or two key villains with the capacity and desire to teach and inspire others, their peers and the screws. This guy Jagga was of that order.

If I felt fortunate landing two-up in a cell with *him*, I can assure you now, *he* was the lucky one. At the mercy of every lowlife south of Bristol is by far and away one of the most uncomfortable places to be, if you happen to be a high-ranking, plain-speaking, non-violent, intelligent, curious and enterprising black gangster from the north. Especially if you also have a taste for the weed. On meeting his equal in intellect and ambition (that's me by the way), he secured himself protection, entertainment and a regular and reliable drugs supply. So my new relationship was hardly one-sided. As the prison became more overcrowded, the friendship became three-sided when Bob Mckiswick joined us. Bob was a decent man, a failed criminal, middle-aged and classically grumpy. In return for a few blims to keep the terrors at bay, he carried our cannabis around the prison for us. This meant both Jagga and I could expect to be released on time, with good behaviour, without fear of being attacked by no-marks or dobbed into the screws for holding.

Jagga was dealt with before me – he got a couple of years and was sent to Dartmoor. Whilst I was sorry to lose him, there was also that understanding that any movement at all was a step closer to freedom. Movement is progress, time served, gone, done with. Before he left, he threw the cell Bible at me. "When you get bored," he said, "see if you can make any sense of that." He hadn't been able to, he admitted. He'd tried the Koran, and that, too, he found wanting. When you're banged up, there is more time to wonder and so there's a greater hunger for a deeper connection, a God if you will. But for a man of crime who scores himself and others on their credibility not gullibility, then the holy books seem to act as guards, not gates, to God's wonderland.

I did as Jagga suggested and put some time into reading the Bible. "Do not trespass" is the message I got, because I couldn't make sense of the scripture. "Come on then, God," I said out loud in the cell. "Come on then, if you're out there, *show yourself.*"

No shining lights. Nothing.

No need to waste any more time on him.

***

They held me on remand for three months, during which time they repeatedly tried to convince me to drop the charges against the police officer who smashed my jaw in. There was no hope of me ever dropping the charges. My solicitor was quite clear – they would have to pay and pay well. I was looking forward to payday.

I left Exeter to serve the rest of my eighteen-month sentence in Channings Wood Prison. I knew half the lads banged up there and so felt quite at home straightaway. The time passed fairly quickly.

Just before release – I was in the pre-release centre, looking down on the prisoners exercising in the courtyard – I spotted Alistair Salmon. He'd not been in for long but I knew he was already being bullied and getting stick from all quarters. He was an ex co-burglar of mine. I'd been told he spent all his time winding everyone up by offering to pray for them. I shouted down to him...

"SAM! SAM! YOU'RE MAD. YOU'RE MAD!"

He came up to see me. I sat down with him. I was as blunt as a spoon.

"What's going on with you? They're all sayin' you've lost it. That you're mad."

He was embarrassed, a little on the defensive. He was reluctant to speak, but eventually he blurted it out...

"Well, it's just, you know... well I had an encounter with Jesus. I'm with Jesus now," he said.

This guy had been out on the rob with me in Holland. He'd been with us when I broke Lydia's nose. He'd joined me on many a burgling expedition around the South West, and it has to be said, he was hardly the kind you'd expect God to take much interest in.

"Oh yeah. Right. Have you got some coffee I can 'ave? You're mad,

Sam, that's all I can say."

And that was it. I just left him to it. Alone with Jesus.

***

My second daughter Tara was born not long after the first, a year, and not long after my release. She too escaped the "predicted" Down's syndrome and was born, full term, a happy healthy little girl. She was another reason why I had to get back out and find some cash, sharpish. But this time it would be different. Jagga had put an idea in my head and now it was turning into something of a plan. I'd invest my earnings in drugs.

After I got out, I hired an XR2 and kept it for three months. I went out every day, robbing, when and where I could.

Alistair Salmon carried on being a Christian when he got out. He went on and on about it. He'd met some Christians in Callington and he went on and on about them too – ruining a good party we were having round at my mum's place.

"Stephen, we'd better get out of here. I can't stand to listen to him."

We blanked him for a while after that – then one day he comes round to see me with a beer in his hand. Asking me for a smoke on my joint.

"What about Christ then?"

"No God any more for me. I've given up on him."

We went out on the rob together then, every day. Still in the XR2. At one house, we were upstairs, I was going through the jewellery boxes whilst he went through the drawers. He found a Bible. Then he looked at the walls. There were pictures of saints everywhere.

"These are Christians," he said. "I can't stay here. I gotta go."

"Well you go," I said. "I don't give a damn if they're Christians."

That night, he asked if he could borrow the car. He brought it back, bashed in, all over, as if he'd done it on purpose.

He'd hit a row of petrol pumps all down one side, before spinning around to hit them again on the other side. Then he'd driven straight back out the petrol station the way he'd gone in, causing chaos and a near fatal accident in the bargain. Thanks for that, Salmon."

CHAPTER 11

I decided to try my luck further afield to get as much cash as I could, quickly, and so started working with Jim, who I'd first met many, many years earlier in Parklands, the kids' home I got sent to the first time they ever put me away. I was only in there for the one night, but even in that short time I managed to make a firm friend of Jim, and after that we'd bumped into one another fairly frequently over the years.

Jim was a victim of the care system. An angry man, he had tons of brothers and sisters, but he was the only one his mother couldn't manage. She was a dark one, his mother, a witch. She used to spit on coal and throw curses at you. She cursed him with a short temper. I paid no mind to Jim's tantrums on the job, as I didn't like to be distracted from my work. If he started a fight in a pub, I'd leave him to it, or if he lost his money in a payphone, I'd wait until he'd finished kicking his way out of the phone box before risking a conversation with him, which it was important to still do, and as soon as was reasonably possible so as to get his mind back on track, to get him back to work so to speak. Taking this attitude with him meant his displays of drama were limited, curtailed, and as he came to realise, quite unnecessary. I was a good influence on him.

I'd decided to ditch driving for a few weeks, and instead, we set off on a rambling and camping expedition. I quite fancied spending some time in the big outdoors. I needed *rambling* gear though, so I went shopping to buy all the latest kit – I wanted it to feel like we were going off on our holidays. I bought a good tent, sleeping bags, haversacks, waterproofs, walking boots, the works. I got Lydia to drive us up to North Devon and she dropped us off in the middle of nowhere. We looked like geography students, harmless. We strode along public footpaths, through villages and up and down private drives pretending to be lost when we needed to be. It wasn't as successful a trip as I'd hoped, to be honest. We eventually made our way back down to Newton Abbot and took a train to Teignmouth and started work again, looking for likely sources of treasure to plunder.

On reflection, I think Lydia was something of a saint putting up with me going off like this and leaving her with the kids. The fact is, I never negotiated with her or took her point of view. I did what I had to do and she understood that. She never tried to change me or my mind. Importantly, she'd always known not to. From famine to feast, she was constant, grounded and as committed to me as I was to her.

Every night we were out camping, I rang home to see how she was and how the kids were getting on. Fine. Always fine. But on this one night...

"All right, Lyd, you OK?"

"Yeah, well sort of. We've had visitors."

"Who's that then, the Old Bill you mean?"

"They've turned the place upside down. Found your torch and your scales an' everythin'."

"What d'you say?"

"I told 'em you used the torch on the cars and yer Rambo knife for fishin', but he didn't believe me until the other copper came downstairs and recognised me. He's the one who 'elped me fill in my application form when I was gonna join the police, remember 'im?"

"Well that was lucky."

"He told the copper that I was all right. An' so they left me alone. I didn't know what I was gonna say about the scales."

"Did they nick anything, that's the main thing?"

"One of 'em went through Tara's nappy, made me take it off. I don't want the kids getting dragged into all this, David. I just don't."

I could hear there was sadness and anger in her voice. I couldn't laugh that off.

"I'm sorry, Lydia. I'll make sure it won't happen again. Did they nick anything?"

"Nothing. Made a right mess though."

I hated to think of her having coppers crawling over the house. Crawling all over the kids as well. It made me want to go home to protect her, but sadly that couldn't be. I had work to do.

***

We slept in fields, not campsites. We kept a low profile. No fires or stoves. No people. I enjoyed being in the big open space, but given the amount of time away from home, we didn't do so well at all. I decided to head for the sea.

So then we were in Teignmouth trying our luck. We found a private road of big houses, all quiet and quite promising. We started at one end and worked through. After doing each house, we stashed our treasure by a tree at the end of someone's garden, the plan being to keep the haul together so we could ram it all into our rucksacks when we left. We were upstairs going through the bedrooms when we heard the sound of several cars crawling over the gravel driveway outside. Coppers. And *loads* of them.

Red-handed, we were pushed into the back of a cop car and driven away, the stash found but the owners not owning up to the fact they owned the goods, which probably meant they didn't. Because they didn't claim the silverware, we couldn't be nicked for it. As a result, I got a result. Two months later I was back home with Lydia.

I still hadn't done much to take my drugs project forward. I knew I didn't want to faff about dealing with the small fry. I would go into the venture at the top end, for top returns. It was high-risk I knew, but that, for me, made it all the more attractive.

With the potential to exploit a network of contacts that could increase my investments substantially, I knew I'd need Jagga on board to make my prospects of success more likely. I went up to Dartmoor to see him.

I never did any bird in Dartmoor, and I count myself lucky on that score as it's all doom and gloom up there, in the nick and out. Princetown is a screws town, and the jail a remote outpost set in a sparse bleak mist pit. Haunting and haunted, they say.

The visiting room is small compared to Channings Wood, on account of the fact the prison is so inaccessible and not many people can be arsed to go there. I could get there in less than half an hour, driving like a loon of course.

Jagga was pleased to see me as he never got visits. I did him a favour and expected one back. He obliged. He gave me the contact I'd been waiting for and he organised it so I could collect a bag of drugs, laid on, which is to say, I could take the drugs, sell them and pay the dealer later on.

Smashing. Even better than I'd thought. Should have come sooner.

***

I went up to Manchester with an accomplice, G. I went alone to the Brown Bear in Salford, on Chapel Street. It was dog rough in there. The bloke I met was unremarkable, donkey jacket, greasy hair, too many rings on his fingers. There was very little in the way of a conversation. I supped my orange juice and left. I met G, gave him the whizz and a lift to the train station. I managed to sell all the drugs within a few days and

I made a handsome profit. I returned to Manchester the following week to buy a load more, and some.

It became a regular job, and it certainly beat climbing up and down drainpipes for a living. I was able to buy everything the kids needed and more besides. I had cars coming out of my ears. I was buying cannabis, E's and speed mostly. I was buying so much I used to arrange for the dealers to go up to Manchester and meet me up there, to pick up their load and be gone with it. On some weeks I had up to four people coming to collect off me. One guy, we'll call him Gary, got invited to join in, on the strength of the fact that when I was nine years old he intervened and stopped all his mates from battering me. He was mates with our Stephen. To return the favour, years later, I let him come up to Manchester and score with me. So he actually met my contact. A few weeks after that, I got a call from Jagga. He'd been released and was back at work. He rang me to tell me that this Gary had only gone up there to score some E's on us own without my permission.

"What d'yer want me to do then?" said Jagga. "His head, his knees? What? I can serve him dog vitamins if you like?"

"Dog vitamins'll do it, thanks, mate."

I've never liked violence – I only ever used it in self-defence or revenge. Pro-active violence wasn't my game at all.

Gary paid £4,000 for his vitamins, and even after that, I still let him buy drugs off me. I've never been a vicious man at all really.

Jagga being out of prison increased and improved my prospects significantly. It was Jagga who introduced me to Paul Massey, Mr Big, and it was Jagga who positioned me for the amphetamine job in France.

Paul Massey at that time was a bit of a gob on a stick, and frankly a liability. The faster we could extricate ourselves from his operation the better, was my thinking. Jagga felt the same. But in the first instance, for an international trade, we needed him. He had millions.

With just one trade, we could earn the money and contacts to finance our own venture that in a few short months would bring us hundreds of thousands of pounds. I'd be a millionaire very quickly.

There wasn't a shadow of doubt in my mind.

Lydia, who'd put up with me working away, getting put away, living on feast and famine in turn, would at last get the security and certainty she needed. She'd brought those kids up on her own really. I wanted to be more of a father to them. Once this job was done, I'd only ever be away briefly but for big money.

CHAPTER 12

I'd be earning enough to give Lydia, anything and everything all the time. And my two children would want for nothing. It was 1989 now – and I was on my way, at long last.

I took my ex co-thief along with me – Jim. He would be my fixer.

I've always liked to work abroad, the glamour of it. I spent so much time in Europe, up to all kinds. I remember Amsterdam as favourite – just the lawless feel of the place. It felt very much like a spiritual home for outlaws. Whilst my friends would often take their comforts from the many prostitutes who sat shamelessly in their windows, touting for trade, that particular form of entertainment had never appealed to me. A reprobate I was, yes, but I still believed in the purity of marriage, and I had vowed to stay faithful and true to my wife, always. And I have.

I'd brought drugs back from Amsterdam before, lots of times, but for personal use more often than not, not that the risk of capture was any less for those without more lofty ambitions. If you import any amount of drugs, you go down, end of. Getting through the port with them is one thing – getting home intact quite another. The last time I'd ended up with a broken jaw. My case against the police was still ongoing. Whilst I still figured on a result and a handsome payout, I could have done without the injury and the waste of energy spent pursuing justice.

Our plan now was to import six kilograms of pure amphetamine destined for distribution across the UK. The drugs were to be brought from Amsterdam by a woman who planned to meet up with us in France. At the meetup, I'd direct my two mules to take a half-share of the shipment and disappear in different directions, giving me two opportunities for a successful import rather than putting all my eggs in one basket.

Jim and I set off for France from Plymouth. We parked our Ford Sierra in the bowels of the ferry and went straight up to the restaurant deck to wait. Wait for the boat to fill up. Wait to see the coast of Plymouth disappear on us. I was used to waiting, cool about it. You have to be if you're a drug dealer. Things don't always go to plan. We'd scheduled five days to complete the mission and just getting to France took twelve hours. Then there was the organising, getting, waiting, moving, exchanging and back again. That's if it all went to plan. And if it didn't, a lot more waiting no doubt, until we got word on what was going on. Back in the late eighties, communication was tricky; there were no mobile phones – well not for the likes of me there weren't. Saying that, my man in Manchester had one – I think the only mobile phone in Moss Side at that time. I wanted one myself, and an RS Turbo, and my own house with a garden for the kids to play in. A few more deals under my belt – big ones, and I'd be there. I knew it. No problem. I was on my way. Well I thought I was.

"This ship movin' yet, Jim?"

"Nope."

He was struggling to read the menu. He held it close up to his head, and because he spoke quietly, I could hardly hear him.

"...time is it now then?"

He didn't answer. I'd already asked him five minutes earlier. He did that sometimes. Took on a kind of "dad" role. Not that we were especially close. He was a business contact, that was all.

I didn't look at the menu for long. I was going for my usual, garlic king prawns to start, steak Diane main. I don't know why Jim struggled so much to read things, whether it was a sight problem or he just couldn't do it. I didn't like to ask either. He always ordered what I ordered anyway. He wasn't that fussed about food. If I'd lived on biscuits for a fortnight, he would have gone along with it, and without a murmur. He wasn't daft or a lesser man than I was. I wouldn't have had him come along with me had that been the case. He was just easy, easy-going. And shit hot when it came to money. On the ball. Did big sums in his head very quickly. And he didn't like to spend much either, not like me. He kind of reined me in a bit – as I say, a bit like a dad, but quiet, cool, calm. So calm, he didn't budge a muscle when four coppers marched into the restaurant and headed straight over to our table.

"James Millington? **** Street, Plymstock?"

"Might be," he said to them, still squinting at his menu.

"Hope you haven't ordered yer dinner yet. Shame if you 'ave, coz you're comin' with us down the station. Get your stuff."

"Sorry, mate," said Jim, putting his menu down. "I better go with 'em. It's a fine, is it?" he said, looking up at them for the first time. They nodded. "I ain't got nowt on me," he said to me. "I better go." Quiet like. As if he were doing them a big favour.

'How much you after?" I asked the copper.

"Five hundred pounds."

"No problem," I said. "Here. Take it." I never carried a wallet back then. I always had too much money to stuff into one. I kept bundles of cash all over, in every pocket. You could have made a few quid following me about for a day, as more often than not I left a trail of notes behind me. I counted out five hundred pounds and offered it up to the coppers.

"He'll still have to come down to the station with us."

We were, by now, the focus of attention for every diner on the ship. Not what you want when you're just going off to do your biggest drug deal ever.

"How long's that gonna take?" I asked them, politely.

"Well, now we've got the money, not so long I shouldn't think."

They were as good as their word. Half an hour later, under a blue light, they brought Jim back to the ship. He walked into the restaurant, sat down, picked up the menu and carried on with his struggle to read it, using his finger, like he was trying to find the place where he'd left off...

"How much champagne you drunk?" he asked me when he finally put the menu down.

"Only the second bottle. You ready for some?"

***

We carried on drinking champagne, eating, bought a few tapes to play in the car for when we got off the ship, nipped up on deck to take some air, smoke some spliffs, and finally got into our cabins to sleep our way to Roscoff. On arrival, we went straight to a hotel, a good one, and carried on sleeping. By evening, we were wide awake and ready for Roscoff. We had to kill time until the girl who was bringing the drugs to us from Holland made contact. How much time we didn't know. Waiting again.

Roscoff is a town of many roundabouts, and between Roscoff and Morlaix there are long-sweeping dual carriages which I took full advantage of, driving as fast as I could, so town to town, I managed, with practice, in just under twelve minutes. We ripped along the road in this fashion every day, and everywhere we went. We rang home from time to time to pick up messages – messages from the girl. As we razzed our way round Roscoff and beyond, we listened to Chris Rea's "Road to Hell" over and over, blasting it out full whack but singing our version over the top of it, even louder, *"We're on the road to jail"*.

I could only cope with these risks we were taking so long as I remained subliminally aware of them. Too aware and you can get paranoid. By repeatedly making the point that we quite possibly *were going* to jail, I was kind of reminding myself of the need to remain vigilant. Even though I was having the time of my bloody life, this *was* work, and as such, attention to detail was always paramount. And so I deployed strategies as a matter of course, to reduce my level of risk and maximise my opportunity to escape, should things turn sour. Even today, when driving, I always leave enough space between me and the car in front, so I can, if necessary, make a quick getaway. It's a force of habit now.

In Morlaix, we settled on a particular bar that had a good atmosphere and a jukebox and we went there every day for beer. The owner of the bar drove a Jag, had it parked there, right out front. Not bad. We got talking. I explained we were staying in Roscoff, waiting for relatives to come and join us before setting off on a tour.

"How long does it take you to get to Roscoff in that?" I asked him.

"Twenty-five minutes," he said.

"I'm doing it in twelve," I told him.

"But that's not even possible," he said. I love that. I love doing what's impossible.

We weren't doing so well on the eating front, and I like my food, so one day we stopped a young bloke in the street, hoping he could point us to a decent restaurant. If we could wait a couple of hours, he said… he'd show us the best restaurant in town. And whilst waiting, we could go to the best pub and have a drink. He jumped in the car with us and took us on a tour. We ended up across the road from where we were going to eat. There was a pool table in the bar so we started a game. After half an hour or so, our new mate introduced us to a few of his mates who'd just arrived. We had the crack for a bit. I liked them so much, I thought I'd ask our new mate if he wanted to come and eat with us – him and a couple of his mates. I was feeling generous. I felt in my top pocket for the thousand pound roll I'd stuffed in there, but it was gone. Gone.

I looked at these French guys differently then. I figured they were trying to have me over. I got hold of him, the guy who'd taken us there.

"Oy you. You nicked my money, did you?"

The men looked at us confused. I pointed to my pocket. "You nicked my money, did yer? If I find that money on you, I'm gonna fuckin' batter you. You got that? I will smash your fuckin' head in."

The men grouped together. I went to find Jim. As I did, I felt in my back pocket and found the money I'd accused them of stealing. We just left then, quick and sly, embarrassed. I was never the jumpy kind, certainly never thought of myself as being, but looking back, maybe I was – a bit. We'd been waiting on the pickup for nearly four days now.

The couriers didn't know they were working for me, although one of them, Matt, *was* known to me. We'd worked together once before. He'd helped to reunite me with some jewels I'd robbed from a shop in Bruges. Originally, it had been a job just for me and my co-burglar, Jez. We robbed a shop, got the jewels but were chased off at the last minute. So we had to bury the jewels in a forest and get out of the country fast to avoid capture. This we managed to do. We drove to Luxembourg, ditched the car, took a train to Roscoff and travelled back to England by boat.

After a couple of weeks, we decided enough time had lapsed to risk going back for the haul. It was a toss-up as to who would go and dig the jewels up, Jez or me. I won the toss and so Jez went, but to make doubly sure that we'd get the jewels through customs, we hired Matt, the ex-security officer who dipped his hand in the bag. I'd confronted him about it, but he wouldn't fess up. So when this drugs job came up, I got Jim to front up as the boss. He paid Matt to travel from Calais through Dover with a cache of jewels in his car – if he'd known it was drugs he'd have refused. To my mind, if he did get caught, he deserved all he got. And to make sure I knew exactly what was going on, I also had someone at the docks, watching out, waiting on him to disembark.

The other courier was also known to me. He was "*Midnight Express*ing" his parcel through Plymouth, leaving Roscoff the day *before* we planned to return home. There was nothing to link this man with us – nothing but loose talk that is.

The amphetamines had been bought and paid for previously by the big man's big man up in Manchester. They would sell on the streets for nearly half a million pounds. I stood to earn a good chunk of that.

So, every day, in the Jag cafe, we were waiting. The big man and his big man were waiting, as were the two couriers, Jim and me. And then eventually she showed up. I'd imagined her in a beige mac with sunglasses and shiny hair. She was one of the ugliest women I've ever met, to be frank with you. She turned up at the bar, bag in hand.

"There she is," I said, standing to greet her. "Come and sit down. Have a drink. What would you like? I should think some champagne might be called for?"

"Champagne? Are you joking with me?" Her accent was strong. "I VANT to get out ov here and NOW please."

"OK, OK." I hadn't been expecting this level of fear and anxiety. I was calm, enjoying myself. I'd spent five grand already and had another two more sent over. I'd got to quite enjoy our little trips round Morlaix and I'd got to know a number of the better restaurants. Being away from home was doing me good. I felt rested. On holiday.

"Sure. I'll let yer get on with it then."

Jim and Karin left the bar and went off to do the business. Jim put most of the drugs in a sealed container in a car that was parked half a mile around the corner. I had organised the building of the sealed container myself so I knew it was quality. Jim then made a series of phone calls back to England to set up the handover to both the couriers, and within six hours we were rid of any evidence connecting us to the crime. All we had to do now was go home and collect.

By the following morning I knew that Matt the thief had cleared the docks in Dover but *"Midnight Express"* man had been caught, stitched up more like, as a kind of bonus ball, a fall guy to keep the drug squad off the scent. I couldn't be sure of it, but it always did strike me as a bit odd to include a walker into the mix, and now I had to hope and pray he wasn't singing too loudly in the cells. So far so good. I'd still be paid well enough for all my work – that was the most important thing.

I sat at the table on the restaurant deck of the ship going home with my garlic prawns and steak Diane all gone, and just empty champagne bottles staring back at us.

"First thing's the RS Turbo. Then a mortgage, right away. An' I was thinkin'… yer know, about the money an' that… What about you, Jim, you got any plans?"

"Just tryin' to *'old on to* my missus at the minute, to be 'onest with yer."

"What's up then?"

"She's gone all weird on me."

"What d'yer mean, weird? Weird in what way?"

"Oh I dunno..."

"Any more from the bar, sir?"

"Yes, please, some more champagne, and can we have clean glasses please? These have gone a bit greasy now."

"That's six bottles already, David?"

"And I'm feeling good. Go on, what were you sayin' about your missus? What's weird?"

"She's been readin' the Bible and... well, I suppose the weird thing is..."

He hesitated, like he was slightly ashamed to be talking like this. I didn't know if he was embarrassed to be talking about his wife or the Bible. Right then, I didn't really care. There wasn't a happier man on that ship at that moment in time. My next job would be E's, going for up to £26 each, at the time. And there'd be thousands of them. I stood to make twice the amount I'd made on that first trip. I was on my way to becoming a very rich man.

"Jim, if you want to talk about the Bible, you go right ahead."

"A lot of what's in it, well it feels like it's true, yer know. D'yer know what I mean? Like..."

Much of what he said went right over my head. I'd sunk at least six bottles of champagne, probably more, but truth is, I wasn't that drunk. After we'd got through eight bottles, I could still hold a reasonable conversation without slurring my words. Of course, I wasn't the most clear-headed I'd ever been, but I wasn't off my head. So when I heard a voice in my head – a still small voice – I was awake enough to listen.

"David, do you really want this life, or do you want to know me?"

By the time the ship docked in Plymouth, my world had changed forever.

STILL SMALL VOICE

New Testament

STILL SMALL VOICE

CHAPTER 13

The minute I got off the boat, I called Jagga to tell him I was jacking it in. He asked why of course.

"Because I want to become a Christian," I told him.

You can imagine the silence. I gulped it down. I'd actually said it out loud.

When the Dover consignment arrived, I took it over to Cornwall for safe burial, until it could be collected. I wanted someone from Manchester to come and take it away. They came and went. Job done.

I didn't tell Lydia about the voice, not right away, but she knew something was up. I was pacing up and down a lot.

Prior to organising the trip to France, Jagga and me had swapped cars. I can't remember why. Anyhow, he wanted his back. He wanted me to drive to Manchester. He wanted to hear the declaration of my newfound Christianity straight from the horse's mouth.

STILL SMALL VOICE

Lydia

We went up to Manchester to pick up a car and collect some money. But the money wasn't ready for us. David left me sat in a pub in Moss Side, being looked after by men with guns. I was sat there for six hours. When he finally came to collect me, we still couldn't go home. We had to go to a block of flats being guarded by some more men with more guns. I stayed outside and didn't ask what he was up to – I never did. I didn't want to know. An hour or so later, we drove home, off our nuts on vodka and speed. The girls must have been at my mum's.

It was on the drive home when he told me that he'd decided to become a Christian.

"I heard God, Lydia."

"What d'yer mean, you 'eard 'im?"

"He spoke to me."

I just laughed. I mean I laughed hard and for a long time. He told me he was deadly serious, and the more serious he was trying to be, the more I laughed – we were off our nuts, yes. But I think I was also a bit nervous – he didn't backtrack, crack or give way. He really was deadly serious.

Trouble is, when David gets an idea in his head, he sticks to it. But I thought no, no, that's not him. He was too set in his ways. He liked the high life too much. He liked his drink, his joints, his speed, new clothes, going out to eat all the time. As soon as we got home, he phoned up Jez and told him we didn't want anything more to do with him or the business. He told them to keep all money due to him. He told *me* it was bad money. He didn't want me or any of his family to ever touch bad money again. That was just the start.

He sold everything in the house, everything, furniture the lot. He didn't ask me. He just went and did it. It had all been bought with dirty money. We had nothing left to sit down on. Fortunately, my sister had just bought a new settee so she gave us her old one. He got rid of all the video tapes and the CDs. Chucked them all out. He even stopped listening to Chris Rea – he had sung the soundtrack to his old life. Bad life. Gone. He does still listen to Bob Marley mind, but otherwise, he changed completely.

Well I have to admit that all this pissed me off at first. I smoked back then. I used to go to bingo. He went on at me, "You shouldn't be doing that". I didn't smoke tobacco until I started smoking joints, and I didn't start smoking joints until I met David, and now he was telling me I couldn't smoke?

People coming to the door selling stuff, shoplifters, he sent away. I think people thought he'd gone mad – but they didn't get on at him. Our friend Alistair Salmon became a Christian and he was ridiculed mercilessly, blacklisted you could say. His friends wouldn't talk to him any more. They took the piss out of him big time. But they never did any of that to David. They respected him. Perhaps they were worried he'd change his mind and remember what they'd said to him. Respected or feared? Who knows?

From never bothering to even notice what stuff cost us, we went to living on £23.50 a week – dole money. Out of that David took ten per cent as a tithe to the church. He'd give them a fiver sometimes.

My dad was thankfully willing to dip his hands in his pockets. He liked David as a person but he had never liked the fact he'd leave me at home, fending for the kids alone, never knowing when or even if my husband would ever turn up again. He didn't like what he did. He said, "Lydia, he never looks after you." He never supplied any backup plan when he went to prison. My dad was a Catholic, so when David became a Christian he got to like him. He managed to change my dad's mind. At first, like everyone else, he just thought he'd gone mad – didn't believe it. But then the change in David stuck – and that brought my dad around to him.

My dad was brought up in a Catholic nunnery in an orphanage. He wasn't overly religious but we were brought up to know right from wrong. He was strict like that. But he always stood by us.

After he found God, I went to church with David all the time. I got dedicated in the church with him. We got baptised together.

I didn't ever start rows with him about going to prison because I knew what I signed up for, but do you know what, I didn't row with him about God either. When he got sent to prison, it wasn't a shock. I accepted it. I stood up for David all the time, even though it was against my family values. Even on the way to the church, getting married, my dad had tried to stop me getting married to him. But we fit together too well.

We've been married thirty-five years this August, and we've had three major arguments, I would say. We have bickered, that's all. I might say, "I don't agree with you doing that", that sort of thing, but nothing major. I do know that if he hadn't become a Christian then we wouldn't be together now, I wouldn't have stayed with him. A lifetime of prison visiting? I couldn't have done it to the kids.

Brian

I became a Christian in February 1989. I'd only been a Christian for a few months when I met Dave. I was selling insurance and mortgages. The Christian house group I went to was just around the corner, a small DIY church basically. The house was in the Grove, Molesworth Road. There were about thirty people there, all told. We took over the place. It was Sybil's. She was in her seventies and lived on her own. Her sons were away, married. The house group was led by a gent called Vic and a lady called Beryl. The meetings were on Thursday evenings. Dave must have met these two and they invited him to the group.

The evening would open with a prayer and introductions to any new people. There was a fella who played the piano. He'd been playing it for years. The meeting was held in both the open lounge and the dining room and we'd all sit around on chairs. Following worship, there'd be a few words of prayer and finally a chat at the end of it. It would start at seven thirty and it was supposed to finish at nine, but more often it'd be ten o'clock. Sybil was frightened of some of the people that came because often, she didn't know them. They were drug addicts and alcoholics. But we kept an eye on them for her. When David came to the house group it was nothing strange to see another outsider coming in. Our friendship grew from there.

I got to know David over that year. I've always liked him because we talk the same language. I just accepted him for what he was. We are all sinners and we all need Christ. We all have a past. But when you give your heart to Christ, if Christ has forgiven you, then that's between you and Christ. At first David was very vague about his history. Didn't tell me much at all at the beginning. As he got to know me, he started opening up.

Truth is, I envied David his past. When I came out of the army, I wanted to be a mercenary. David had lived the life that I'd always aspired to – full of excitement, being your own man, having wealth, having the strength of character to make dodgy decisions and come through. He was someone people looked up to. So *I* had no problems accepting him – I know for certain I'd have done what he did, given half a chance. Not now of course – before I found Christ.

David

Martin my brother came round and couldn't believe how we were living.

"David, you've got no bread an' butter even. You can't live like this."

I waved my Bible at him. "This is enough. It's enough, Martin."

"Can't you stop it with that Bible, David, and talk to me." *That* was Lydia.

"This is what Jesus wants!" I told her, time and time again.

She's the best wife. She'd put up with me as a villain and now she had a Christian to get used to. And as we all know, the converts are always the worst.

One of my first ports of call was the local church, the church I'd got married in. I went round there and explained to the vicar – the same vicar who'd visited me in jail but now had shorter hair – that I'd become a Christian and that I wanted to join his church.

"Come right on in, my son. You're welcome."

I can't deny I didn't feel uncomfortable the first time I went to a service. Guilty too, when I thought back to the times I'd melted down the Lord's candlesticks with a torch. There were only about eight people at the first service I went to. I took Lydia with me and some two pence pieces from a jar I used to drop change into. But even this offering was tainted. All the money I'd ever earned was tainted.

Lydia had been brought up to go to church so it wasn't so strange for her. She'd sung in choirs even. We just sat down and kept ourselves to ourselves. Yes it was uncomfortable, but at the same time I could feel the Holy Spirit guiding me. I felt at peace. I sat in church and prayed for peace. I felt as if I was being lifted up. I wasn't doing this under my own steam. I couldn't have. He, the Holy Spirit, had hold of me. From the time on that boat, to this day, I have felt him. It was stronger back then, perhaps because it was new, but I still feel the spirit and it's always been strong enough. Alone, I could never have given up my life of crime.

Alone, I could never have faced the villains down and told them I'd found God. Alone, I could never have foregone opportunities to earn large amounts of cash. I could only do it because the Holy Spirit was with me.

Brian

I only used to meet him at the house group for the first few years, I suppose. He was a regular. He was very keen to learn music. He loved his guitar – still does. He got involved in the *Timothy* programme, which is based on the two books of Timothy in the Bible. Timothy was one of Paul's evangelists, someone people used to look down on. Paul wrote letters to Timothy instructing him on how to behave and how to look after himself - how to win people over. He taught him how to preach the word, because Timothy was timid – he needed to be courageous and to trust God more. So David went on the *Timothy* programme in 1990 or 1991, and he loved it. After it, he wanted to go to Bible college. Lydia his wife would have gone with him, but then things happened in David's life which meant he couldn't go. David said the Lord had told him not to go.

David

Alex Salmon's face was a picture when I told him I'd gone Christian. He didn't laugh or disbelieve mind. In fact, he advised me to leave the church I was going to and head down to the Plymouth Christian Centre instead, in Cattedown, a district on the edge of the city of Plymouth. I ignored him.

One Sunday at church, a few weeks into my new life as a Christian, the Holy Spirit intervened. It was just after a service. I was watching the old people drinking tea. They seemed to be up on a kind of stage – projected – separate from me. I didn't hear a voice exactly. It was guidance, I thought. I felt as if I were being guided by the Holy Spirit, and the message was – *"Not here, David – go there. Don't want you here. Just go."* I was happy and wanted to stay in the church I got married in so I didn't want to hear this message at all – but I listened.

I felt it only fair to let the priest know my intentions. He'd wed me and welcomed me with open arms as a member of his congregation. So I made my way to his house. He lived at the back of the church behind an arched gothic oak door. As soon as I knocked, he was there. I explained that the Spirit of the Lord had directed me to attend church in Cattedown.

"That's Elim, isn't it?"

"Elim?" I said. "What's that? What does that mean?"

He slammed – and I mean slammed – the door in my face.

I later found out that Elim is a branch of the Pentecostal Church, but I didn't know a Baptist from a Methodist back then. It was a whole new language for me.

The Plymouth Christian Centre had a big congregation. More than three hundred people. On my first trip there, I met Kerry Jackson – or rather he came over to me. He immediately warned me off. "These are good people, David. There's nothing here for you. And please, leave the safe well alone."

He was an old Swilly kid. We were in the Swilly riot together. He knew me well. I can still see the look on his face. He kept saying it. "These are good people, David."

I told him I was there to see Jesus and went inside the church. I followed the service, blending in and making my peace with God. Over the following weeks, it became regular for Lydia and Jim and his wife to come too. Jim had seen the change in me and he wanted some of it.

So there we were, the four of us, every week, for months, going to church on a Sunday.

***

My family had to live on tomato sauce sandwiches. We didn't even get to keep all our dole money to live on. I took 10% a week to pay a tithe to the Christian centre. Lydia didn't kick off about this. She accepted and trusted that in time things would get better and improve. We were as one, still.

Shortly afterwards, I went on a church workers' course. The Plymouth Christian Centre had set up a Bible college at the tabernacle. Only certain people who were interested went. It cost about two thousand pounds, which the church paid for. It was an eighteen-month course squashed into a year of study. Intense. For someone who had never managed to study before, it was *very* intense. I loved it. Every day, I walked from Swilly, or North Prospect as they'd renamed it, to the tabernacle at Cattedown for my class. I fasted too and not just because we didn't have money. I was spiritually hungry and fasting helped me to focus my mind on the Lord, who I knew would feed my soul. So I would regularly fast and pray. Fasting alone is not conducive to spiritual enlightenment. The intention of prayer, of communion with God, needs to be there also. If Lydia cooked a Sunday lunch and I was fasting, she could be a bit off with me. "I don't like it when you're fasting," she'd say. But for me, it was an opportunity to deny the flesh and be at one with the Lord.

I went on like this for a whole year. Most mornings and evenings, as I walked through North Prospect on my way to and from Bible college, I knew that the locals were sniggering behind my back. I was told. They all thought I'd gone mad. Lost it. Taken too many drugs. Couldn't find my way back. Of course, I remembered the day I'd called out to Alistair Salmon in Channings Wood Prison – "You're mad". I never sniggered behind his back mind. I *screamed* it straight into his face.

It's very difficult to convey the manner in which God and I

communicate. I don't want you to think I'm mad, that's why. I know when people say they hear voices, this is the usual diagnosis. I wouldn't say that I hear voices, rather I hear the word of God being spoken to me. I get messages. For instance, when I first started reading a Bible, I used Lydia's, a small white book of the New Testament. When I started Bible college, they told me there was another Testament, an older one. They gave me a new Bible with both in, and this one was easier to read than Lydia's – the NIV, the New International Version. But then one day at church, one of the men came up to me with a Bible in his hands – it was the old King James version. He said, "David, I've never done this before and I don't feel comfortable about it, but God told me to give this to you."

Without all the *thees* and *thous* in it, the NIV was far more palatable to me and so I carried on reading with it. Not long afterwards, there was a bang on the door at home. Our Martin had brought me a Bible, ripped, battered and with loads of pages missing.

"Budgie said to give you this," he said.

Budgie was a Swilly boy who had got himself locked up in jail in Morocco. The Bible Martin brought me had kept Budgie sane in jail. He died young, but back in England, in Torpoint, the other side of the Tamar from Plymouth. All this Bible activity happened within the same week. And then Lydia went to America – a holiday gift from her parents. She returned with a present for me – a Bible. Yep. A King James Bible with huge writing. I got the message. This was the Bible God wanted me to read. Once again, the Holy Spirit had intervened. I know I'm not mad.

Three months into Bible college, we were brassic. I was happy. I was doing OK. I was managing my studies. Lydia spent a lot of time round at her mother's – they were close. The girls – Jade was four, Tara three, still babes really – they didn't really know or feel any difference. Lydia did. She'd stopped banging the doors and flying off the handle but she still seemed burdened by the poverty.

Some days we *didn't* have bread. There *was* no milk or margarine in the fridge. Nothing. We were in just such dire straits the day I got a call from my solicitor.

"David, you're up in court in two weeks. You're to be awarded compensation by the police for the injuries you sustained to your jaw. I'm just glad they've finally settled, as I know you'll be."

This was the light at the end of a long dark tunnel.

But then the Holy Spirit intervened again. I heard its still small voice.

"David, I want you to forgive the police officers who broke your jaw and drop all the charges. Don't go any further with it."

And I thought, "Right. OK." But I'm thinking, "You sure about that, Lord? Really?"

I decided to get help. I knew a guy called Bruce Taylor, a solicitor and Christian who worshipped at the Plymouth Christian Centre. I went to see him and explained that the Holy Spirit had advised against me claiming compensation.

"David, if you didn't provoke the attack…"

"Well, I was speeding and then I stopped and then these two officers beat the crap out of me and broke my jaw in several places…"

"If that's what happened, then you're entitled to your compensation. However, if you say God has intervened and advised against the claim, then I must leave it up to you to decide. Legally, you're well within your rights."

That was no help at all.

I went home and told Lydia.

She didn't go mad. She'd been living on broken biscuits but all she could say was, "David, you do what you gotta do."

I went to see my solicitor. "David, I don't know for sure but you're likely to be awarded anything between fifteen and thirty thousand pounds."

"I don't want it."

"They'll go mad about this you know. Two police officers have been sacked. [I never knew that.] Thousands of pounds have been spent on legal proceedings. And now you say you want to drop the charges." He was dismissive. Far from doing the right thing, he saw my change of heart as an annoyance and disruptive. "They won't just let this go, you know. This isn't the end of it. You'd better write a statement. Have a word with my secretary."

She was elderly, grey-haired, old school and equally unimpressed. "So why are you changing your mind?"

"Because Jesus told me to."

On the statement form, she wrote down that I no longer wished to pursue a claim against the police, ending with "because Jesus told me to." And then she looked me dead on, in the eyes.

"Sign here."

So there was no payment. No comeback. Nothing. I carried on getting fifty quid a week and tithing a tenner to the church.

***

One of my first attempts at making some money was as a window cleaner. I could fit the work around my studies and get some much-needed cash in hand – honest cash that I declared for tax purposes. My business was called *Heavenly Windows*. Of course, the people of Swilly and the Plymouth police force figured it to be a feeble scam – a ploy enabling me to recce houses prior to us burgling them. They simply could not believe that I'd gone straight. They could not believe I'd found God.

One afternoon, I was out on a round on the same street as a Halfway

House where, at that time, Alistair Salmon was living, not long after his release from another stint in Channings Wood. Now it was me who the Christian. I saw him come out of the house and shouted over to him. We walked to meet each other. We were standing in the middle of the road.

"You in there again, I see?"

"Not for long," he said. "We're off to Holland. We've 'ired a *Porsche* this time. We' ain't comin' back till we're rich."

"Sam," (short for Salmon) I said, "Sam, come with me. You found Christ once, you could find him again, I know you could." He was standing one side of the white line in the middle of the road, I was on the other. "Look, Sam," I said, "you've got a choice to make. You either choose Satan an' go an' take your chances, or you choose God an' come with me. S'up to you. What you gonna do?"

I couldn't have been more blunt. He looked at me with a pained expression on his face. I was the mad one now.

"Nope. I'm gonna go with them," he said.

So off he went to Holland. A few weeks later, they came back in the Porsche and he was no richer than he was before. Probably driving under the influence, he had a major road accident which put him through the windscreen. Amazingly, he only broke his nose – but quite badly. They put him on morphine to help him cope with the pain. He decided to supplement this medication with drink and drugs and managed to choke on his own vomit and die.

I carried on cleaning windows for a living.

Chapter 14

I think it's fair to say that after becoming a Christian, I started to "feel" things. As a young criminal, I hadn't felt anything much at all.

I hadn't felt for my victims, that's a fact. I didn't have the capacity to internalise what I was doing, to others or myself. Christ changed all that.

Lydia was pregnant with what I hoped would be our third child, and this seemed like the best present that God could have given us. But this would turn out to be Lydia's fifth miscarriage. Even now as I talk about it, my eyes fill. The loss was almost unbearable.

I suppose feeling can be a good thing too – I felt the Lord to be with me. I felt the Holy Spirit uplift me. But I felt the loss of our child so deeply, I was inconsolable. Perhaps it's as well I didn't feel the others as keenly, for how much can a man bear? Lydia bore the tragedy with strength and pragmatism, as she had with the others. Her mother was a huge help – her mother had also miscarried children, though she didn't carry the "suspect" gene that was at the root of these tragedies.

A couple of months later, and Lydia was pregnant again.

STILL SMALL VOICE

***

As part of my new life, in addition to Bible college, I went to a house group every week with fellow members of the church. My first time was memorable – it was held at a house in Stoke, Plymouth. It was a large Victorian house with a huge lounge with dividing doors leading into another very large room. There was a circle of antique wooden chairs stretching its full length, so enough seats for at least twenty. What struck me about the place was the smell – it was an old person's smell – mustiness. It took me right back to my burgling days. This was the smell that used to greet me climbing through a window, coming off the net curtains, the old wood, worn leather, musty carpets and polish. At this house, there was a French carriage clock on the mantlepiece with a double button and repeater. And a set of silver candlesticks. I couldn't help myself. There was even a piano in the corner.

I am a twenty-five-year-old ex-gangster, standing at over six feet tall, but sitting amongst a gaggle of little old ladies, feeling like Moby Dick out of water, balancing a cup and saucer in one hand whilst eating a biscuit with the other.

"Would you like a hymn sheet to sing from?"

I was tongue-tied.

Ken started tinkling the ivories – singing commenced. *"Be brave, be bold, the Lord thy God is with thee. People, be strong, for the Lord thy God is with thee... I am not afraid, no, no, no. I am not afraid."*

The Elim Pentecostal Church is a gospel church, and so my fellow singers were loud, animated and full of passion – as was I. And this was still only a month after I'd heard the Lord my God speak to me for the very first time.

Churches across Plymouth provide support for the homeless, with soup runs being mobilised every night all across town. Our church did Friday nights. I felt something for homeless people so I volunteered to help out and then became a regular. I felt humbled by the work – a feeling that was alien to me.

The soup run operates with military precision, but this good order and organisation is just a cloak for the wealth of love and kindness that is the real sustenance being offered to the destitute in the city's streets. As well as love, there was home-made soup we'd pick up from a woman who made it year in and year out, plus we'd get donations from all over, so there were pies and pasties donated by *Oggies*. We got shoes and socks and blankets, tea, coffee, bread, fruit. We'd assemble in the huge kitchens above the church and heat up the pies and pasties so they were mad hot. Then we'd wrap them in silver foil. Then we'd get a bag and put other bits of food in, some crisps or biscuits, enough for one person. We'd make up bags like this and then get out there, four of us, working to a rota, starting at 9 pm, Charles Cross Police Station lay-by, then moving onto Bretonside bus station, and afterwards, the wedding cake shelters up on the Hoe. Before they'd shake hands with the down and out, the needy, some of the volunteers got the antiseptic spray out first – bit harsh, I thought. After handing them their stuff, they'd spray again to make sure. But I soon learned they were wise. One night, a man shook hands with me and I immediately felt the wetness coming off him. I had to look down and see. I knew it'd be grim. What exactly was I shaking hands with? He had a finger missing – it was a fresh wound. The bone still sticking out of it. I ran for the spray myself then.

They weren't all homeless. Some came out of their own houses and then went back to watch the telly once they'd been fed. I still felt privileged to be a part of it though, to hand over much-needed warm food to cold old men and women who we found on the streets, huddled under blankets, starved, and at the mercy of the elements. One night we fed an old man who spoke so posh, you just knew he'd experienced a sheer and shocking fall from the grace of his younger self. He sat beneath a huddle of blankets, keeping the wind off and the occasional smattering of a cold shower of hailstones. It was bitterly cold to be out on the street. I noticed something move under his blanket. My fellow Christian spotted it too.

"Does your dog want some dinner? They get hungry too you know?" He motioned for the man to remove the blanket so the dog could be fed.

"That's not my dog!" said the man. "That's my wife." And he slid away the blankets to reveal the wretched sight of a little old lady, eyes closed, cheeks sunken, barely alive I thought. This was a side of life I'd not considered before. I was deeply moved by it.

If I think about feelings and things that affected me in that sense then I think about Flo. She was an old lady living homeless in Bretonside bus station. We parked the van up and Lydia went up to her as she hobbled along, finding a place for the night.

The old lady came hobbling back down with us and got into the van. Lydia gave her her last dinner. And then she walked back up to the station with her blanket and a bag of food to lay down on a bench and get off to sleep for the night. That was it. But what happened then? After that, this bloke came along and tried to take the blanket off her, but she wouldn't let it go. So he stabbed her in the neck with a knife. Killed her just like that.

When we heard it on the news, we phoned the police. They'd asked for witnesses. "Yes, we've seen her. We gave her some food. We gave her the blanket."

The police came to see us both. Took my DNA, which they never had before, took mine and Lydia's fingerprints in the kitchen, and then took our clothes. And he said – I can remember him standing here now, "We're going to keep your DNA. You know that then?"

Yeah. And they kept our clothes as well – the usual thing, for six months, eight months, whatever.

In those four years of doing the soup run, there were lots of circumstances like that. Bare and painful poverty exposed to the elements.

And feelings come with it. You know, you're feeding the old lady, you're feeding children. You're feeding people. You're looking after people. And then the next minute she gets stabbed in the neck. I suppose it's the hopelessness of thinking of that little old lady and trying to help. You know what I mean? She actually had a flat and she had a family, but nobody was helping her.

The family didn't really want her – they rejected her. They didn't look after her. So then you think... right... OK... how can we get you off the street? There's a lady that we had good contact with – Major Shirley Collins of the Salvation Army. So you see her and say, "Look, what about this lady?"

"David, we do know her. If you can get to her, do, because she won't talk to us."

So then you start talking to her, and if you can get into talking, you can say, "There's this place you can go to."

"I don't want to go there," she'd say. And so you *could* have taken her off the street, she *could* have got off the street. If she'd wanted to.

You could, you could try, but sometimes people won't listen or don't want to, or whatever the circumstances are. And they stay on the street – that was her, Flo.

You're doing the soup run right, every night. And when we come home, like, I don't know what time we got home…one o'clock, two o'clock in the morning…depended…now when we got back, first we'd do the dishes in the church and then we'd get back home and get into a nice hot water bed, warm water. The bed is heated. So you're getting into it and you think, fancy being out there now. Poor sods. I mean, whatever you do when you're out there, you try to help in some form or another, feeding them or providing blankets or whatever else you can get hold of. Anything useful, we'd take it. If and when I tried to do more, go further, I had to contact Major Shirley first. She was the overseer. You could go to her and say, "Oh, do you know somebody who could help out with this person, I found sleeping here?"

"Yes, I can. But will she go into this place? Here's a phone number." And Flo could have gone and got some help this way, but she wouldn't. So that's as far as you can go, cause you can't do any more, unless you just physically grab them and drag them off somewhere.

And then the next minute she's stabbed in the neck and she's dead.

So that's the hopelessness of it – I just couldn't help her.

It was a bloke who came to the soup run asking for food – a ginger-haired boy. He stabbed her for her blanket, got caught, and was done for murder, and he's in prison to this day.

If I hadn't been doing the soup run I wouldn't have known or cared. But now that's the thing about the love of Christ, what he gives you. When you know him, it changes you inside. You have that love, which he's got. You can try and help somebody as much as you like, but if they aren't going to receive it, then you can't do nothing about it. But you don't expect them to get murdered.

And then there was Mark Brown.

Mark Brown meant more to me really. He worked in the Kentucky as a manager and he loved his grandad and grandmother. They both died within a year and then he lost his job cause he couldn't stop being depressed. So then his wife left him and he was out on the street. So he's gone from managing the Kentucky with a wife and kids, and because he got depressed and lost his income, it's all gone.

Now he's on the street and he's drinking, and I find him on a bench, frozen. Then I phoned through for food and a blanket. Maybe it was Shirley again.

"What do I do about this chap?" Like, you know, this is what he's doing.

She said, "We do know of him and he will be back here tomorrow, David, so I would say wrap him up, keep him warm, give him some food and make sure he's OK."

I've done that, and I thought, well, I don't like that, so I'm going to go back tomorrow. I went back in the morning and took some paracetamol and water because I thought he'd be hungover.

"I can't take a paracetamol, I'm not allowed, but I'll have the water though."

So I said, OK, so I'm talking to him. And that's when he told me what happened in his life. He'd been beaten up. They took him to hospital and found maggots in his open wounds; he had a cut in his chest and the flies had landed there. So then we have week after week, month after month, still seeing the bloke. And I'm thinking he's going to deteriorate and get worse. And then they said, "Oh, we've got a vulnerable adults meeting, would you like to come?"

So I said, "Yes, I'll come."

And there's like police, social workers, everybody around this table, and I'm listening to them all. And I went, "Um, can I say something?"

"Who are you?"

"I've been on the soup run for four years. This is a vulnerable adults meeting, right? That bloke is like the most vulnerable person I've ever met. He had maggots in his chest. He's back on the street. If you don't take him off the street now, he'll be dead before winter."

And he went, "Well, there's nothing we can do about it."

I said, "I don't understand. You've got a vulnerable adult. Why don't you put him in Glenborne or somewhere like that? I don't get it?"

They said, "We can't, it's up to him."

Right. "Vulnerable adult means he's vulnerable. And he can't make his own decisions."

And he can't and they left it. And then at the North Hill Reservoir someone kicked him to death. He was killed in the reservoir on North

Hill. They just took his money off him – whatever change he had on him – just really for the hell of it. I mean, he's homeless, they're homeless – they just started kicking him and didn't stop until he was dead. He wasn't in a good state and he just didn't care any more and said, "Dave, I don't care if I die. That's why I'm drinking like this."

You've just got to live with them things, haven't you?

Brian

When Christ gets you, he gets you. He takes your sins. That's all in the past then. I was forgiven so why shouldn't David be forgiven? That's what Christianity is all about. "Forgive them Lord for they know not what they do."

Oh, of course, you could say, "Well it's a bit convenient!" It's a bit handy to turn to God when the going gets tough, but the fact is that if you don't truly believe, if you don't give God your heart and give up sin and turn righteous, life won't improve any. You'll forever be saddled with doubt and disappointment, shame and fear and all the rest of it. Once you give your life to Christ, you live a life blessed with joy and promise. David is the happiest man I know despite his troubles, and even now his troubles are many. I for one don't know how he copes with what they've thrown at him.

I look back on my old life now and can see that money was my God back then, not Jesus. And I accept that. My life has changed dramatically since then.

Like David, I've not been free of temptation since joining the church. I have been sorely tempted, truly. I cheated on my wife when I should have known better – but in November 2002, I wanted to kill her. I had my children with me in church and I was so angry at her and her boyfriend... me, the killer. I was going to use a shovel. I was crazy, and when I finally made the decision to go and get her, the Lord said to me, "You do it *your* way Brian, or you do it my way." I turned around and walked back to my children.

If I'd done it my way I'd have ended up in prison and never seen my kids again. My ex-mother-in-law would have ended up looking after them. I couldn't do it because I had the Holy Spirit inside me – it's a powerful thing. David lives and breathes spirit.

In 1993 David approached me to help him set up in business. He was applying for a Prince of Wales funding grant and so he approached me to help him draw up a business plan. Which I did. He presented it to the Prince of Wales Trust and was given £5,000 to start up. I went to work with him – stripping furniture.

We were stripping a lot of doors. He had to get some practice in. My missus would say, "Don't take my doors, don't take any more of my doors!" We worked in a shed in David's back garden. We mended tables and chairs and all sorts. We got on OK but fell out in the end – though not badly. I just couldn't work with him any more. He'd make crazy decisions without me. He'd ask for advice, I'd give it him, and then he'd go off and do as he pleased.

For example, one week we were asked to strip somebody's car chassis. And David said, "I don't want to do this." So I said don't do it. We ummed and aahhed and then we both agreed that if we were going to do it, we'd need £120 minimum. So then David said he'd do it for fifty quid. I said, "I can't work like this." And so I left him – we parted ways. When he needs some advice he'll come to me. He listens and then does his own thing. I love Lydia, I love David to death. And my friendship with him is all to do with Christ. I had to leave him to it – but we've remained friends ever since.

I believe when David told Lydia that he'd found God, she was high on drugs and just laughed at him. The temptations for David – they must have been so great back then. But we know the Lord doesn't ever give us anything we can't handle. Some of the temptations and pressures and challenges that David's had to face? Only a faith in God could keep a man like that from violence. I know people he would've killed. He tells me how hard it is. He tells me that he struggles when he feels like doing something bad, but then he talks to the Lord and it settles him. If it wasn't for David's love of Christ, some people on this planet wouldn't be alive today.

Whilst we're firm friends, we're not in each other's pockets. He invited us to Cyprus for his daughter's wedding. We shared the château with him. Lydia was very poorly at that time. He paid for the lot. We had to actually fight our way to pay for the hire of the car. He's such good fun to be around. And he likes to travel – that's the truth.

In 2007 I was working for BT as one of BT's top salesmen and won a five-star all-expenses-paid holiday (to Singapore and Malaysia). I asked my ex if she wanted to come with me. She didn't have a boyfriend at the time. She said no. So I went with David. When we got there, they all thought we were gay. But they soon found out we were born-again Christians. We stayed in the Fullerton Hotel in Singapore and the *Four Seasons* resort in Langkawi. We had a great time. Everything was free. They even gave us money to spend and we actually came back with more money than we went out with. David had a great time. We felt it was a gift from the Lord.

He's still in his backyard now – working really hard, bringing home the bacon. However, it's not all plain sailing – on the contrary. He's put his life and soul into that business but the local authority has been doing its level best to close him down. I've never seen him so angry.

It's OK to vent and get angry. Jesus got angry with people selling gold outside the temples. He turned their tables over. It's how you handle the anger – that's the trick. But what he's going through right now – not sure how much or how long he can deal with it.

No one can deny that David is a changed man, and to be fair, his is the only Damascene conversion I've ever heard of. I've been in the church a while now and seen many come and go. It's very rare for sudden converts to persist with their righteousness as long and as well as David has. Even in the Bible there was only one conversion as dramatic as his – and that was Paul.

But how long will it last if God keeps testing the strength of his conviction – pushing him to breaking point.

David slips up now and again as we all do. He may not read his Bible for some time. When you go to church regularly, when you pray regularly, when you worship regularly, *you are with Christ*, like you're in the fire with Christ, you burn with fire. When you stop going to church, stop reading the Bible, stop praying, stop worshipping – that fire goes cold. You go cold on Christ. What you need to do then is get back in the fire. Get hot again. We all go through that. David is no exception. I've been through that. Some people slip back because they've got a history of drug abuse. Or they've been alcoholics. They just slip, slide back. If you're in the fire, you're close to Christ. You benefit. It is peace. Everything in life is just peaceful. The world may be throwing everything it can at you, like all this stuff with David and the council. This has been going on for five years. I've supported David over those years as best I can.

David is a strong character. If he thinks he's right, and even if he thinks he's wrong, he just won't turn away.

All his children visit his house every day and all his grandchildren come with them. Every day. You've got to be something special for that. And I think he would have done it that way even if he wasn't a Christian. He loves his children and all his grandchildren.

David is a good and faithful servant. When his mother died I went to the funeral and I spoke to him. He was clearly very upset. But his mother had made a commitment to Christ, and at one point in his life, so did his brother Stephen.

Lydia

We were living in Whitleigh when the fifth one miscarried. I was sixteen weeks gone. The day before, I'd lost some blood and so went to the hospital. They scanned me and couldn't find a heartbeat, but that didn't mean the baby wasn't well. They told me to go home and come back in a week. That night, I remember waking up because it felt like I'd wet myself. Both of us were covered in blood. It was horrendous. That was the first time David ever saw a miscarriage, and it was a bad one.

Tara was born in November 1987, Jade in 1986. Only eleven months between them. After I had Jade I had more miscarriages. Before he got Christ, he would just disappear, go off. Deal with it in his own way. He never came home. And when he did he'd be drunk or stoned. He never talked about it. I knew it affected him though.

The worst was one – I was eighteen, nineteen weeks gone. I was in bed. The doctor had told me to lay up and relax. My mum came out and looked after the kids and David. Well, he was really supportive. He was there then. And when I lost it, he came to the hospital with me. Afterwards, we gave our son a naming ceremony and called him Cody. A couple of friends from the church came along too. The doctors told me I couldn't carry boys. Which is weird. They said the boys were affected by Down's syndrome and the girls weren't. Katie was about eighteen months old then.

It felt so much better that one – even though it was the worst. I think that's because David reacted completely differently. He was there, he never left. He sorted the kids out. And Jade, especially Jade, she was six or seven and blamed me for losing the baby. "You killed my baby," she used to say. So Davey took her camping. And he talked to them. And he wouldn't have done that before.

I liked seeing that different side to him but I loved him so much anyway. Nothing would have or could have changed the strength of love I felt for him. I'm not saying I wouldn't have left him – I would. I told him that once the children were old enough to ask where he was, once they missed him and had to go to prison to see him, then I'd leave. I vowed not to be one of those mothers taking their children to visit their father in prison month in, month out. *I* didn't mind going but I didn't want to bring my kids up to think it was normal.

Jade was four and Tara three when he became a Christian, so he got there just in time, I'd say. I've often wondered if, subconsciously, he gave up being a criminal on account of the kids. But I don't think he did. He might have contemplated the idea. He knew if we did split up I'd never have stopped his contact with the kids. He'd never have lost them or lost touch with them.

Now when I think back, I realise I used to pray more than I let on. I used to pray he'd come home when he'd go out for a pint of milk and he'd be gone for two years. I'd pray for us to be a normal family. I prayed for that a lot. To have a normal family, like everyone else. And now I've got one. My prayers have been answered.

It's not been easy though. When everything – and I mean everything – changes, you feel like you've lost control. In actual fact we were much more "in control" but we had far less to get control of. Less food for instance. Before, we would have eaten out every night. We'd go to *The Lanterns* every night sometimes and just eat what we wanted, as much as we wanted. We ate steak, beef, the best of everything, at home or out. Then it went to sausages and fish fingers every day.

Before he was a Christian, Jade knew she could have anything she wanted. He would come back with prams and dolls – anything she asked for. He was still the same after. He gave her what he could, but none of it was stolen. And as ever, he still gave them the love.

Lis

My name is Lis and I am fifty-four and I've been in Plymouth for eighteen years and I've been in the house I'm in now for seventeen years, which is opposite Dave. We witness his daily battles with carpentry and his grandchildren and God knows what else.

We met Dave the day we moved in. He was out on the street. He was fiddling with wood – he's usually fiddling with wood when he's on the street. We met Dave and we met the Masons, another family who lived two doors down. I think Dave came over and introduced himself as a neighbour. I'd actually seen him several weeks before when I came to look at the house. I'm a firm believer in the flow of life. I'm not religious in any way. I don't believe in organised religion. I don't believe there is a supreme being looking down, being malevolent or benevolent. That's just insane. Maybe I'm wrong and when I die I'll get a poke in the eye, but we'll see when we get there. I believe in the flow.

We decided, because we liked Plymouth, that rather than rent we would just buy a house. I knew nothing about Plymouth then and I didn't know that Swilly had a bad name. I know – kind of gives it away, you'd think. They call it North Prospect now.

We'd got a short-term let on a house in Saltash, just over the Tamar Bridge, whilst we were looking for a house to buy. I liked the first house I looked at, in Cookworthy Road. It was big and square, so I arranged a second viewing so my partner could see it. Driving back to Saltash, I got lost and ended up on the Swilly estate, in Wordsworth Road, outside the house I eventually bought. I had to get my A–Z of Plymouth out to see where I was. And this guy walked down the road with a shaved head. I thought "hooligan". He looked all right. Dave was going into his house with his brother Martin, like a pair of shaved monkeys. The house directly opposite him was for sale and I bought it.

I saw Dave again on the day we moved in. That's when he came over to introduce himself.

He was all right, very friendly, well a bit chatty as it goes. I said, "Sorry, bud, I'm busy. Chat to you later." A week later we went to the local social club and Dave was in there with Lydia. The Masons invited us. We got pissed and got to know each other better then. And it's kind of spiralled out from there.

I thought he was a really nice guy. I see him every day. I discovered he was a Christian fairly early on. Back then, he was still fairly rabid and enthusiastic about his conversion, evangelical, trying to spread the word. We'd have drunk conversations and swap stories. I talked about my move from London and all that, stuff about drugs and how I was glad to be away from it all. I knew he'd been a bit of a speed head, a bit of a freak for it, so I kind of knew he'd been a bad boy. It's just the way he is in himself. He is very confident in his body. I can spot people who are capable of looking after themselves. He was no football hooligan though – he didn't even like football. He's got a diamond of a wife – poor Lydia practically brought them girls up on her own because he was in and out of nick all the time. I was with someone like that once myself. So Lydia and I would swap prison stories. I know exactly what it must have been like for her. Sunday best for prison visiting and all that. It's just stupid, but you do it because you love 'em, even though you hate yourself for loving them.

I'd get a little bit of info from here, a little bit from there. And so, piece by piece, I could build this bigger picture of David, the man, before Christ and after. I've never had any issues with Dave.

I hung around with the old-school criminal fraternity for a long time when I lived in London. Proper old school, with rules and codes. Dave was very much like that. He was a villain, a rogue, and so we got on famously – apart from the God bit. He used to bore me shitless sometimes, but I'd give him as good as he gave me – we had and still do have, major theological debates. I am spiritual – don't get me wrong. I wake in the morning and say thank you. Because I like being alive, and I've been close to death enough to really know what that means. I'm a firm believer in what I can feel. But I don't and can't believe in a monotheistic God.

David

For a whole year I walked the several miles each way, every day, to go to Bible class, so I could learn from my holy teachers. That was hard work in itself. I like to drive.

My childhood school days are barely memorable, but of what I can remember, I know only that I was never good enough or clever enough to warrant the attention of the teachers. The subjects they'd taught didn't interest me much either. So now, here I was, a changed man. As a Christian, I'd developed a powerful hunger for knowledge, for learning, for receiving the wisdom that would and did help me manage my future and the future of my family. I was so earnest.

At one of the Bible classes, it was announced that the church would fund several places at the Elim Bible College in Nantwich, up in the north-west of England. After the course lasting several years, I could then become eligible to work as a pastor. This appealed to me immensely, and so I was invited to visit the college in Nantwich for a three-day introduction to the course, prior to moving up there with the wife and kids.

The college was magnificent.

There was a nursery for the children. The grounds were beautiful. They would give Lydia meaningful work to do. I could concentrate on my studies, surrounded by people with passions as fervent as mine.

Whilst I was visiting the place, someone had a birthday. One of the priests took up a guitar and the whole place revelled in song and praised happiness. It felt so right. It felt so perfect. A world away from Swilly and the low aspirations of my childhood – now, I could look forward to giving my family a future bright with possibility. I could immerse myself in my studies without the worry of how to feed the children. The light couldn't have been brighter. But then the Holy Spirit intervened. Again.

"No, you will not go to the Elim Bible College. You will support yourself and your family in Plymouth."

I was devastated. Even now, as I remember it, my heart still delights in what might have been.

Instead of Bible college in Nantwich, I went to a standard College of Further Education in Plymouth to learn carpentry. In my early days, I'd lied about learning welding at night school, now I was learning off my own back, for real.

I suppose I knew that any work I did would have to be manual. I didn't have and doubted very much if I'd ever have the confidence to take a desk job. I could manage Bible study in class, but to take on work where people were relying on my ability to use and write words? That would have been a problem.

Lis

I think he is amazingly tolerant and patient and compassionate with his kids and grandchildren, even to the point of it being detrimental to his own relationship with Lydia and his own health sometimes. I think he is a lovely man. My only concern for Dave is that he seems to be filled with sorrow and regret sometimes. When he looks back on his life, he hasn't quite got the idea that who you are now is a product of where you've been. He hasn't quite realised it is OK to be at peace with your past.

I don't think he's at peace with his past. I think he's regretful. He says he is easily appeased, but I don't think so. I think he's sorry that he's been naughty and he's been away from the kids and has put Lydia through the ringer and all that stuff. I think he regrets it. For example, he always qualifies a statement with a "I know it's really bad". And I'll say, "Is it really bad?" It wasn't bad at the time when you did it. You've got mental capacity. You were in full possession of all the facts but you still did it. You made that choice therefore it was the right thing to do at the time. I'm not a believer in retrospect. Hindsight is a cruel teacher. *If you knew the future, nobody would do anything. You wouldn't try anything new. You wouldn't be curious. I don't want to know my future.

Dave is constantly with his kids and grandkids – all the time. The grandchildren, he loves to bits. If you want to have a dictionary definition of a doting dad or a doting grandfather, then just put Dave there.

He loves them with all his being. It is sweet – I wouldn't put up with it – I couldn't do it, but it's lovely to see. I couldn't cope in his front room for more than an hour because it's just too hectic. I can't do with screaming girls. And they all are screaming girls. We call them the goblins. Especially the triplets. They are a nightmare. Absolute nightmare. "Grandad! Grandad!" Bless him. I often wonder if maybe this whole conversion thing is an after-effect of love. I know this sounds kind of weird. It's almost as if he came to a sudden realisation that he had nothing in his life. And maybe that's kind of part of it. I don't know. I don't have that religious fervour. I don't have the conversion experience. I've heard stories from my dad and my mum and I've heard stories from Dave. Dave believes he's had a deeply religious experience.

He was chasing money. I think when he was on that boat he somehow realised the only thing that mattered in this life was Lydia and the girls and that he couldn't lose them. I think that sudden realisation is what changed his life. And God just provides a framework for the shift. A ready-made script with boundaries and rules. I think Dave is on the autistic spectrum. And those boundaries, reasons and explanations are very useful for someone with autism. But who am I to pooh-pooh his ideas – whatever floats your boat? I am high-end Asperger's. I know because I took a client to a clinic to get tested and the client wouldn't do it, so I did it, went first like. I scored higher than him!

STILL SMALL VOICE

Tara

The first memories I have of my dad was when I was about three or four. He was very interactive and playful. We used to play shark games – dragging the sofa out and hiding. And we used to have "Dip" nights. They were family sessions. We'd get the front room table out with lots of food and dips and stuff. No TV. No nothing. Just a "Dip" night. He was always very interactive with us kids – very *there*. I remember going to his workshop in Connaught Lane in Mutley. Him making pigs and cows out of wood for us. His friends used to make us "Christmas houses". We went there a lot. Actually, sometimes I used to hate it. He used to drive me mad. "I do want to do some work," he'd say.

He was very strict. We weren't allowed in other people's houses. When we were younger, we'd get very angry about it. We could only go to certain houses for tea with certain friends. But we couldn't just walk around randomly. We weren't allowed sleepovers. We were allowed at my nan's, Dad's mum. Dad was the baby. The golden child. They were very close.

He was always very close to his family, but we didn't see his older sister until we were about eleven – the one that went to South Africa. I'm close to all my aunties and uncles. Maureen is a funny character. She's always jolly and cheerful. She reminds me of my dad, but a female version. She laughs and giggles. And Steve. I always remember him flitting in and flitting out. I was close to him. I didn't really get on with my nan back then, when I was younger. We only started getting on when I was about fourteen or fifteen. We clashed because we had too much of the same personality, I think.

I always remember Stephen coming round and sorting out our disputes if Mum and Dad were away. Martin, I don't remember much about him when I was younger. He was there for Boxing Days and stuff like that. When he wasn't away in prison. I see him much more now – practically every day. He rings, he comes round. He is also at Mum and Dad's a couple of times a day. He spent half his life in prison and the other half with his mum. He could never be by himself. So now she's dead it's a big change for him. He's trying to find ways of dealing with his life. He's being good. He's on the straight and narrow. It keeps him concentrated. And he walks. He puts sticky notes everywhere to remind him of things he has to do every day. He's a bit OCD, very particular.

Same with my dad. He doesn't like noise. He's like my son. He'll go upstairs and wait until the noise has gone and then come back down again.

David

Not long after I became a Christian, Lydia suffered yet another miscarriage. Her fifth. I had never felt any pain for the loss of the other four. Literally, I mean. I'd felt nothing. Every one, I'd swallowed and then just got on with my life, not thinking and not feeling. I knew Lydia grieved for every one of them, and to my shame, alone. I just never felt that sadness for myself. I'd even been there at one of the miscarriages – I woke up to a bed covered in blood. My response? Same as to all the others – I went out and did some more burgling. I went travelling. I went to the pub. I went on a binge. I never felt anything, ever.

So when she had the fifth miscarriage, I was shocked to be overwhelmed by the intensity of the impact of feeling that engulfed me. The pain tore into my soul, my heart, my world. I was struck by sorrow and grief. Perhaps much of that sorrow was unspent grief for my unmourned children. I don't know. All I remember is the force that engulfed me, a pain so big and a heart so sad – I was forced to reach to the very depths of my imaginings to find a way through it. It was awful. As I write about it now, my eyes are still full of tears. Dead babies are the pits, I can tell you – and most especially when they're your own.

I was learning to become a carpenter when our third child Katie was born. I think it's sad but fair to say that Katie received far more love from her father at the start of her life than either Jade or Tara. I can remember, again with such shame, teaching Jade to roll me spliffs at three years old. What kind of father does that?

I believe I've since made up for some of their losses, but I can't go back and give them the love they needed when they were born. I live with the sadness and the guilt every day and God gives me the strength to manage it, so I can be grateful and giving, rather than resentful, angry and down on myself.

Guilt is, however, still a very heavy word.

STILL SMALL VOICE

Tara

My dad's got gout. Every so often he won't drink red wine or he won't eat steak. He'll go through stages of not eating or drinking certain things. He's very spontaneous, and things can change quite quickly with him.

But I've never witnessed or seen anything to suggest my parents having an argument. They had one once when we were older, but nothing when we were younger. They kept us pretty sheltered from all that kind of stuff. Mum said she used to take us to visit him in prison, but I don't remember that. She stopped when we got to a certain age. He's been very open when we've been old enough to understand what he did. In terms of drugs and everything else, he's been very open with it all. I was shocked at how big his record book was and all the things he did wrong. It was crazy. If there hadn't been a name on that form I wouldn't have known it was my dad. I wouldn't have put him in that category. Just completely the opposite.

My main memories are us going on holidays. "Pack your bags, we've got half an hour." We went to America three or four times. We've been all over Spain and France. We did France, Germany and Switzerland, drove right through. We just did different things. Theme parks and mountain climbing. We always enjoyed a holiday. Driving round. One time, he booked a holiday to the Caribbean and we were all moaning that we didn't want to go. We'd only just got back from Florida about two weeks before. We were brats. "We just want to stay home with our friends, Dad." He liked travelling.

There are still some things he won't have in the house. Nail varnish. We weren't allowed to wear it until we were fifteen. No short skirts or anything like that. Very modest.

David

I got to manage the children at Sunday school. Yes me. They left me in charge of them. We had a fishes and loaves experience one Sunday when there were clearly not enough Jaffa Cakes to go round. But then everyone took one each from the box, and lo and behold, there were enough! The box just kept on giving. There are twelve Jaffa Cakes in a box and there were thirteen of us. I know you will think I'm crazy saying this – but it's true. It's what happened. It's true that Jesus spoke to me often.

I had another more profound experience when God spoke to me at the start of my journey as a Christian. This time, I didn't listen to him. I was walking home from Bible class but I'd told Lydia to come and collect me. I wanted to save her the journey so I started out for home, walking really fast, hoping to catch her. She was driving a white Ford Fiesta. I was very nearly home, and right at the time I knew she'd be leaving. And then God told me to run, not walk. *Run*, he said. *Run fast.* But I didn't think it was God – just my mind playing tricks on me. So I didn't run. And then I saw the car. It was heading off up the main Wolseley Road. Now, if I had ran, she would have seen me. By ignoring God, I'd put my wife to unnecessary effort and wasted her time. But then when I got home, there she was. She hadn't gone anywhere. It was someone else in a Ford Fiesta, one that was very similar to ours. I was confused then. Was God playing games with me? I didn't run and it wasn't her anyway.

A few days later and I'm on Dartmoor with the Sunday school children. We'd taken them out for some exercise and fresh air. It was a fabulous day. The kids went off in pairs and they were given strict instructions to stay on the main paths. Dartmoor is vast, wide and it's easy to come a cropper out there, especially if a mist descends. But on this day, it was clear and the forecast good so we didn't envisage any problems. At the allotted time, the kids started making their way back to the vehicles. By the time we were due to leave, there were still two missing, a boy and a girl, both aged about twelve. We waited and waited. Nothing. I went on the hunt for them. I looked far and wide, nothing. This had to mean they were down in one of the rifts, small valleys that are part of the terrain. So I set off again, panicking, wondering what they were up to. They were old enough to have a relationship and I really didn't want to be the one responsible for letting something like that happen. After about twenty minutes, I heard a car start up. Then came that voice in my head again, saying *Run*. Again. This time I obeyed. I ran as fast as I could towards the sound of the car. As I rounded a gorse bush, there they were. A middle-aged man with the two kids in the back. I jumped on his bonnet. He stopped the car and got out. "I was just going to bring them back to you," he said. I could see in his eyes that he'd had no intention of doing that. I got the kids out the car and held onto them. We walked away. I asked them what they thought they were doing getting into a car with a strange man. "He said he'd take us to the caff for chips." I thank God. I thank him daily. There's so much to be grateful for.

Tara

We had to go to church every Sunday for as long as I can remember – until Mum said we could make the decision for ourselves. I was about ten when I said I didn't want to go. But I changed my mind every week. My girls go to the Girls' Brigade, so they're taken to church on Sundays for that. They go. They lack the spiritual side. But they do go. They enjoy it.

When we were kids, we were completely different to our friends. I felt weird when I was younger. We were called Bible bashers. I used to get all upset about that. I remember telling my dad about that. I think he had a chat with some of the parents and they never called us it again. I'm still friends with them now, them girls, I still speak to them.

Our strict upbringing meant we weren't allowed anything "witchy", but I was very into all that when I was a kid – I liked *Buffy* and stuff like that. Dad hated it. "Spells and witchcraft. The Devil's stuff," he said. I've always been close to my dad. I can talk to him. We'd argue a lot about the father of my kids – when I was seven and a half months pregnant, Dad was so angry about him he punched the TV in – but otherwise, conflict was rare . Punching anything was very out of character for dad.

He loves Christmas – he's like a big kid. Him and Mum would always sneak down first to make out like Santa had just been. Dad would always be there for the present opening, and at Christmas dinner he'd sit up proud with his hat on. He loves Christmas and gets very involved. Halloween was a no-no, mind.

I had many problems with my pregnancy – it was triplets –I had to go to Bristol for the birth. They asked my dad to drive me up there. He put his foot down and said no, that I should be taken up in an ambulance. I got to Bristol at about nine forty-five in the evening, and at ten fifteen they were born by C-section – Imogen, Page and Holly in that order. I rang my dad from the operating table (they were at the Grecian Taverna drinking champagne). I was on the phone to them when Holly was born. They drove straight up the next day.

CHAPTER 15

Tara

As I've got older I've got more religious. Me and Dad have quite a lot of discussions about it. I'm more open to going to church now. I do believe in God. I believe in him more than not believing in him. I've read the Bible, but not recently.

It's Mum and Dad's thirty-fifth wedding anniversary and we are sorting out a surprise party or meal – a "get-together" thing. This will be in the Grecian Taverna. It's hard trying to keep it secret. Dad doesn't like surprises. He doesn't like parties. There'll be about thirty people. Uncle Stephen is coming with his daughters. Maureen is coming and Rose is coming. Gail is coming, a friend of theirs from when they were younger.

I know that Dad will come out with some crazy comments when he does his speech. And he'll start singing. He always does. It's a great thing that he's managed to turn his life around – it'll be a really happy anniversary celebration. They worked at that – together.

The whole family dynamic would have been different if he'd carried on burgling – God knows what it would be like. I'd feel ashamed, I know I would. Dad's very open with the kids regarding what happened, so they can learn from it. I remember once going round the cemetery with him and he pointed out all the people who had died of drugs. To put me off. It worked. The grandchildren have got him wrapped round their little fingers. He still won't let them go round to their friends' houses. He's very protective like that. Kids. With everything else he's a big softy.

Not so long ago, he passed out on the floor in the middle of MacDonald's. It's because of all the stuff going on with the house and the fight with the council. They're trying to steal his house off him because the developers want it. They've tried their level best to make life hard for him, trying to shut his business down, accusing him of stealing his own land off himself. It's been terrible. It's been really hard seeing him suffer so much and for so long. He'll go from being fine to really upset. I read his doctor's notes – he's broken down, he's a broken man nearly. I've never seen my dad cry. So hearing how bad it got – it's really hard. It made me really angry. The whole situation. It's so difficult watching him go through it. He's been so angry he couldn't speak. Won't talk to anyone, not even to the kids. Clams up. Stays in his room for days, his brain ticking over and over and over, trying to get through it. He'll sit there and repeat things. And he's lost so much weight. Lost loads of weight with the stress. He won the case, but then they still had to have a go. They sent him a letter saying they may come back and fight again one day. So they're keeping on at him. But the threats. They've awarded him compensation but they've not paid him yet. They have to go through another judge to get the money. They're being stubborn. Him and Mum argue about it – it was all very tense. Poor Mum gets overwhelmed with it all. We don't need to be worrying about walls in other people's gardens. The stress has made Mum a lot worse. This is not nice. And then the kids pick up on it. If he wasn't a Christian... well I guess it'd be much worse. Him turning to religion saved our lives.

David

It was just a couple of years after I'd found Christ when the neighbourhood watch woman came round to see me.

"So, David, the police are looking for you."

"Really?" I said. "What's going on then?"

She said three riot vans had turned up round the corner. Loads of cops with helmets on, battering rams and dogs. They knocked the front door down. "It was my son-in-law's house," she said. "They threw him on the floor, put cuffs on him and said, 'You're under arrest, David Hills, for cannabis and cocaine.' My son-in-law's into martial arts and everything but he was absolutely terrified. Told them they'd got the wrong house, but they wouldn't have it."

They were at 45 Wordsworth Crescent instead of 45 Wordsworth Road. I went round there and knocked on the door. They still had the guy under arrest at the police station. Some other guy answered the door.

"D'you, uh, do you have the search warrant?" He pointed to a bin in the corner. "Do you mind if I have it?"

"Yeah, take it."

So I took it. Right enough, it said David James Hill, cannabis and cocaine. Now, I've never had a drug conviction ever.

I phoned up the DC named on there. So I said, "You came around my house?" He denied it. "Now let's just cut to the quick. Look, I know you came around to the house because I've got the search warrant in front of me."

He said, "Could you come down to the police station?"

I said, "I'll be down in ten minutes."

I drove down to Charles Cross and they put me into this interview room. I said, "All right then, let's cut to the quick here. I'm a Christian now, right? Not into this life any more. I go to the Christian centre down the road, David Beresford is the pastor. You can go and get a character reference from him if you want, but, um, whoever's told you this, got it wrong." I pointed at the search warrant. "I know it must be someone high up who has given you this information because you wouldn't turn over my house willy nilly, not with that amount of force – without a nod from someone. Not you lot. Trouble is though, God sent you to the wrong house, didn't he?"

And the copper went, "What?"

And I said, "It's funny that you've been coming to my house for the last twenty-odd years. How many times have you been to my house – loads. Never ever did you go to the wrong address. Not once in all them years, but now you've gone to the wrong address. Don't you find that a bit strange?"

He said, "I'm finding this whole conversation a bit strange."

I said, "Yeah. Well, I know that in three months' time, whatever, you're going to come back to my house again, aren't yer? Am I right? But," I said, "my children don't know anything about my life. When they get old enough, I'll tell them all about it. So if you want to come back again, or when you do come back again, *not if,* could you come during school time?"

"In school time?" he says. "You want me to give you a time and a date, do you?"

"Yeah, that would be nice."

"David, as weird as this all is," he said, "we won't be coming back. You'll be the talk of the nick tonight, that's for sure."

And I thought that was it, but then he said, "Can you tell me anything that's going on in North Prospect right now, David? What do you know about all the drugs down there?"

So I said, "No, I can't, but if I did know, I still wouldn't tell you, because I'd be like – how would you put it – Judas… Judas Iscariot." I just wouldn't do that. Couldn't do it. Never would.

And he went, "Yeah, but drugs are evil."

And I said, "Yeah, I know they are. But, uh, like I said to you, I don't know nothing about that. I'm not involved in that, in any way, shape or form any more. But, uh, no, I wouldn't say anything. So, now you know." And off I went – that was mad.

David

I think the trips to Romania were really important, because they were so heart-wrenching. The little girl, for example. I can still feel her on me, even now.

We're in the van, right? On the front, it's got the rainbow charity motif, which I really didn't want. Because it feels like… look at us. We're great. Someone said it would help us get through the borders. I don't think it did. But anyway, off we go. It was mad cow disease at the time.

We're heading to Zeebrugge. There's Jenny, Heather and me in the van. I'm driving up the M5 with two fat old ladies. That's about the best way I could put it. We all stayed in one room. And they snored like grizzly bears. The next night I said no way – I'm going in my own room.

We've gone through customs. I don't know what's going on. We're sitting in the van with eight thousand pounds in cash. And the van was filled up to the gills with all sorts of medical stuff, kids' clothes – I really didn't know what was in there.

So this bloke has come over. He shines his torch. He goes, "Uh, do you have any food, any foodstuffs?" It's the time of mad cow disease, remember.

And I went, "Um, do we have any foodstuff, Jenny?"

"Oh, no, no, no."

And I said, "No, just kids' clothes and stuff like that."

He went, "Oh, OK." And he's gone.

"We don't have any foodstuff, do we, Jenny?"

"Well, we got some cereal. That's all right. We got some bacon because Eddie likes his bacon. Yeah. And we've got some sausages."

"And we got some eggs."

"Eggs!"

"Jams and marmalades."

Everything that we shouldn't have had.

We get to Romania, and just as we go through the border, the officials come out with big pipes of disinfectant, spraying all over the van. Eye-stinging. It was like Jeyes Fluid. Good job they didn't know we had a ton of sausages on board.

We were heading for a small town and we'd been told we'd be staying at a doctor's house. Not a proper doctor. A vet. He was the head veterinary man in Romania – top dog. And we were bringing him a vanload of contaminated sausages. So we're driving along, and then Heather says, "Yeah, it's up here." It's midnight. We're driving up a dirt track. Mud is *that* deep and it's raining hard. There are bombed-out houses to the left and right, and as we're coming up the road, eight blokes all hanging out in a car.

I've driven to the top of the road but it's just a forest, a dead end, and I'm spinning around because the van was so heavy. It was actually better in the mud. The two women don't know nothing, so I'm thinking, put my seat belt on, and Jenny says, "What are you doing, love?"

I said, "Put your seatbelts on, both of you."

"Why?"

What to say. "Well, it's twelve o'clock at night, and we're stuck up a mountain in six inches of mud. We've got eight grand in cash, a van full of kit, and two old ladies in a white transit with a rainbow on the front! When we get down this road, I fully expect that car we just passed to be parked across our right of way – and I ain't stopping, so put your seat belt on."

I just gunned it as fast as I could go. Standing in the middle of the road was a bloke swinging a baseball bat. I just drove through like he wasn't there. He leapt out of the way and I kept driving. I'm looking in the mirror waiting for the car to come after me. I thought with all the weight in the back of the transit I'd spin around. We got away.

When I saw the little girl in the orphanage, she clung onto me like a koala bear. I had to prise her off me.

That was horrible.

I was listening to the Harry Potter author, J K Rowling on the radio yesterday, talking about these orphanages. And she said one of the most striking things that she wants people to understand is that when you go to these orphanages the children will just latch on to you – they'll latch onto anyone in fact, because they want to leave with you. That tells you something about how they're being treated. That they'd rather go with *anybody* to get out of there.

"Do you know what?" Lydia said. "David, you know we would have taken her? And it wouldn't have been an issue." For fifteen hundred quid I could have taken her. It would have taken two weeks if I'd gone back and got her. I could have brought her home in two weeks.

***

I always liked singing without realising I could do anything with it. When you've lived a life in borstals, children's homes, and the like, you're led to believe you're no good at anything. Or if I went to get a job, I'd always think I ain't going to get that job. There's no confidence there. So when I started singing, I just sang in the church praising God, but then I started singing solo songs that were really meaningful. When I sang them, the feedback was like, "That's mad, Dave, what you just sung, you're very, very good."

So I would use my singing, and not just in church, but everywhere, even in a Muslim restaurant. The wife was really mad about it. It was a Christian song, so all the people like stopped and listened, and I'm there singing. In pubs, and I don't mean karaoke places. I just like singing wherever I go in life. I use it.

So then I started writing songs and playing guitar, and I thought, yes I can do this. I wrote all my chords down and took them into a recording studio. When I released the album people rang me up, often non-Christians, like Lydia's sister, and said, "Dave, I can't believe you've done that." She said, "David, your singing soothes me so much, when I feel down I'll go and listen to it. The words you wrote change the way I feel."

When I make music or sing or even if I'm just talking, I like to reflect on the influence of Christ in my life. I like to think of it (and me) doing something good for people. If there's no power in it, it means nothing.

Jesus changed me inside and out. Anyone can do it. You can live your life for Jesus as much as you want or not bother. It's not forced upon you. You can take him or leave him. Give him half your life or all of it. I know the more I give him, the better things get. If I look at my family life now compared to then... when you do what is right, everything falls into place. Jesus changes everything in that sense.

My daughter said when she read my Old Testament, "Dad, it really didn't sound like you. I can't grasp it." And she said, "I think you feel the same, Dad."

I look back now and think God's truth, it could have all gone so badly – but it hasn't. I've gone down a different route.

I have to stop and think. It's been thirty years since knowing Jesus, from the boat, from that car in Moss Side. I think I knew then, where my life was headed. In a very ugly direction.

I heard that call: "Do you want to know me or do you want this life?"

I said, "I want to know you, Lord."

Not in a million years could I have dreamt up the man I've turned into, the man I am now. Look what I can do – the music, the woodwork.

The solid and reliable family man. I have just made three COVID screens for the church and they look really smart. I put my heart and soul into them. And yet I started out by making fifty-pence pieces in school in metalwork. I never had a clue.

When I first worked with wood, I was clueless, to be fair. Somebody from the church gave me some furniture and asked me to dispose of it or do something with it. One piece was a door with a damaged pane. I made three different new panels and none of them fitted. Useless. No good. I felt utterly useless. Who was I kidding? So I asked – prayed – to be shown how to do it. I started with "Heavenly Father", and before I could say Amen, he'd told me how to do it. So I cut the piece how I thought it should go and put it in – absolutely perfect. Martin my brother was there. I said, "Martin, do you believe in God?"

He said, "What?"

I said, "I want to show you something." I showed him the door and asked him which panel did he think I put in.

And he said, "They all look the same to me."

I said, "Do you know why that is? God told me how to fix that."

Sound well cheesey I know – believe me, I know. But it's the truth, I'm telling you.

In the old days, I guess I would have been able to make a baseball bat with a big nail sticking out the end of it. I would have got that much done. And now God has changed all that.

God will give you the ability and the patience to do whatever you want. Now I choose to make good things.

Everything in life can change.

***

STILL SMALL VOICE

LAST WORD

from

DAVID'S PASTOR

(David Evans)

The story you've just read all happened over thirty years ago. Some of you might have the question in your minds "Has it lasted?"

It would be an understandable question: so many of those who start well don't "stay the distance". Today, Dave is a very different person from the person you have read about in the early chapters of this book. But he still has the same sense of fun and a tremendous love for life. After twenty-five years being thoroughly involved with a large Pentecostal church on the other side of the Plymouth, he has more recently worshipped closer to home, here with us at Morice Baptist Church. Indeed, he has been a valued member of our community for about five years now. He has always been very upfront about his past. He has even shown us a list of his convictions, not to boast about his past but to ensure we knew something about his background, where he's come from and how far. He's travelled some distance. Since the events described in this book, Dave has helped on the Plymouth soup run, taught Sunday School, taken aid to Romanian orphanages and now leads the worship group at our church.

Thirty years after the events of this book some of his former "friends and colleagues" are serving long prison terms. Others have not even got that far, having died, sometimes violently. Dave knows that he could so easily have been the one in prison. Before Dave turned his life around, he was on the road to wealth and riches (or to hell in a handcart). By contrast he has now built up a successful carpentry business. He started out working on reclaiming timber and making reproduction Regency, Victorian and Edwardian fireplace surrounds. Now he can turn his hand to all sorts of furniture. When Coronavirus hit, he was especially helpful. At the beginning of lockdown, our church needed to install a series of see-through screens, to shield those leading worship from the congregation, Dave came up with the goods – to buy them commercially would have been well beyond our church finances.

Dave is also a talented singer and musician – he leads the worship in our church and has produced an album of his own songs. (https://music.apple.com/gb/album/embrace/1535468703).

Ironically one of the people who helps to lead the worship used to work for the police replacing locks on houses that had been broken into.

Dave and his lovely wife Lydia are this year celebrating 38 years of marriage. They have three beautiful daughters and eleven grandchildren. Dave's life has been touched with sadness in the last few years with the sudden death of his mother and the death of his brother, while his nephew Calum was tragically murdered in March 2020.

Although this book has been all about Dave, it is about someone else too. The person behind that still, small voice who spoke to Dave thirty years ago has been guiding him and helping him and will continue to do so.

Printed in Great Britain
by Amazon